Life On A Balance Beam

IT HELPS IF YOU DON'T LOOK DOWN!

Life On A Balance Beam

IT HELPS IF YOU DON'T LOOK DOWN!

A Guide To Positive Living In A Precarious World

Paula Statman

Published by

 Piccolo Press

484 Lake Park Ave. #101
Oakland, CA 94610

Printed in the United States of America

Library of Congress Cataloging-in-Publication Data

Statman, Paula
Life on a balance beam: it helps if you don't look down! /
by Paula Statman
p. cm.
ISBN 0-9640042-1-6
98-96571

First Edition

Book design by Todd Crawshaw

ACKNOWLEDGEMENTS

I want to thank the following contributors, supporters, and good friends for their important roles in this project:

Rita Derbas, creative muse and dear friend, for always being there at just the right moment with just the right idea.

My editor, Mary Lou Hulphers, whose unfailing optimism, energy, and keen eye spurred me on to new heights—and kept me from sinking to new depths—more than once.

To Todd Crawshaw, who captured the spirit of the book beautifully.

To Max Dixon, whose suggestions in Seattle came at the perfect time.

To Dr. Bob, who created the room for me to write.

To all of my friends and colleagues, who granted me creative license with their stories, and allowed me to include them in these pages.

To my e-mail buddies, who kept me connected to the world during my days and nights of writing.

To the thousands of women who have enriched my life. It is a joy and honor to share these words with you.

And to Oreo, who warmed my feet at my desk, when the rest of the world was asleep.

Dedication

To my husband, Alan, for his love and support. It takes courage to be married to someone who considers your endearing qualities "good material" for her book. Thank you for letting me hold up our relationship—embellishments and all—for the world to see.

To my daughter, Lauren, who made wonderful contributions to this book. Your laughter inspires me to be silly in front of large audiences.

And to my mom, who can cook up a storm (thank God) and sustains my family in times of need.

CONTENTS

WARM UPS: How Did We Get Up Here?

I am not now, nor have I ever been, a gymnast. In gym class I was the only girl who *patted* the Horse instead of vaulting over it. I knew my limits and wisely avoided sports that involved leaving the ground for any length of time. But today, I love watching gymnasts on television.

My favorite part is when gymnasts "stick the landing." When they finish their routine, flip through the air and land squarely on both feet, it's amazing! I perform a similar feat in my kitchen. I retrieve a can from the top shelf of the cupboard, climb safely off the kitchen chair and raise my arms in victory as my family cheers. (I think they're relieved supper won't be delayed by a trip to the orthopedist.) Sometimes, to dazzle them, I'll carry two cans at once.

Considering my lack of athletic skill and a more than average fear of heights, you would think I'd confine myself to ground level and move *very* carefully. Instead, I live and work on a five-inch wide balance beam, four feet off the ground.

You heard me right—I live on a balance beam. **And so do you.** You may be completely uncoordinated and not even own a leotard. But, it's an absolute fact. If you're a woman, you live on a balance beam. (If you're a man, you live on a golf course, but that's a different book.)

How did we get up here? Some women lifted themselves up. Some brave ones took a running leap. I was air-lifted by helicopter.

◄•••►

It's not easy up here; it's slippery and narrow, and the ground looks like it's a million miles below. But, now that I've gotten over my nausea, I'm convinced that this is a good place to be. Because everything we need to learn is UP HERE.

Living on a balance beam we:
- **stretch and stay flexible**
- **plant our feet firmly before we make a move**
- **exert tremendous energy when it counts**
- **reserve our energy when it doesn't**
- **deal with the things that throw us off balance**
- **gain stamina and strength**
- **fall off, forgive ourselves, and try again**
- **perform with growing confidence**

If you've ever watched gymnasts perform, you might have noticed four qualities in their movements—*strength, flexibility, balance*, and *grace*. Even if you don't aspire to become a world-class gymnast, you still need to develop these qualities. They're not just the foundation for everything you try to do up here; they are essential to finding more joy and satisfaction in your life, your work, and your relationships. In fact, these four qualities are so essential, I've devoted a section to each.

Some of the women you will read about are struggling to stand up on the balance beam. Some are walking cautiously. And then, there are those who are performing amazing moves and are very much at ease up here.

Wherever you are in your own life on the balance beam, I hope you will find inspiration and laughter in these pages.

◀••▶

6 RULES FOR LIVING ON A BALANCE BEAM

1. **Living *on* a balance beam also means falling *off* the balance beam.** No exceptions, not even for Olympic gymnasts.
2. **No need to be coordinated to live up here.** Just get good insurance.
3. **Falling off the beam is a reminder to let go of perfection.** An often *painful* reminder.
4. **Buy a floor mat.** And don't skimp on the padding!
5. **Climbing back on the beam develops calluses.** And resilience and determination.
6. **Leotards are optional.** That's why God created sweat pants.

FLEXIBILITY

Staying Loose And Limber

FLEXIBILITY: *It's A Stretch, That's For Sure*

No woman likes stretch marks. They are, as the advertisements say, "unsightly." But, stretch marks don't automatically mean you've gained thirty pounds faster than your skin could take it. A woman also gets stretch marks during pregnancy, when her abdomen and breasts expand to make milk and room for a baby. Once the baby is weaned and the milk is no longer needed, the stretch marks fade, leaving behind little trace of how the woman had to expand to accommodate that kind of extraordinary growth and change.

Stretch your old and perhaps, negative perceptions of stretch marks for a moment. Instead, see them as "stripes" we've earned in the past decade that symbolize how far we've had to go to make big changes.

Don't worry. The marks will fade with time, but with diligence and effort, what they have allowed us to accomplish, will not.

The following two sections contrast how stretching our old attitudes and behavior propels us forward in society and how narrow thinking holds us back. While the issues presented are typical to mothers, they remind all of us that making real change is a stretch, that's for sure.

WORK AND FAMILY FLEXIBILITY

Unless you've been asleep for the past fifteen years, you've probably noticed that the structure of the workplace has changed. And, some of the biggest changes are a result of employees seeking more balance between their work life and their home life.

Many companies have found it's in their best interest to provide employees with the necessary policies to achieve the right balance. Today, companies that don't offer such policies may risk losing talented employees to more family-friendly organizations. Some learned the hard way that they risk eroding employee commitment by making it harder for workers to take care of personal needs. These same companies are now more willing to do what it takes to keep their employees longer.

Marquette Electronics, Inc. in Milwaukee has a relaxed atmosphere vigorously supported by its chairman, Michael Cudahy. Marquette let its 2,200 employees, including production workers, adjust their own schedules and dress as they wish. The policies and resources that include a child-care center on site have lured skilled workers and helped produce solid earning gains.

Aetna Life & Casualty Company doggedly promoted flexible scheduling even as the company endured five years of downsizing. Though Aetna has cut staff 24% since 1989, the number of employees on flex-time has risen to nearly 60%. Flexibility reduces turnover, Aetna studies show, and there's evidence it also fosters productivity.

In those companies where morale is down, and overtime is up, many employees are afraid to use flexible scheduling and other policies. They encounter resistance from management and are afraid that their careers will be harmed.

◀··▶

But more employers than ever, not only allow employees to seek a balance between their work and their personal life, but also see it as smart business strategy. And some companies like Hewlett Packard favor flexibility programs that are geared to all employees, not just those with a family.

Jerry Cashman, H-P's work options project manager, says requests are evaluated on what impact they have on the business and co-workers "so we don't give it to the guy going back to school and not to the woman who has a problem with dependent care." He said, "We've been a leader on flex-time off and flexible working hours within a day. Now we are looking at flexibility within a career."

Companies like these are the best employers for women in the 90's and beyond.

As essential members of the workforce, we have to show business how humane practices positively affect their bottom lines, so that our options remain open. And, let's continue to demonstrate how employees who "work to live, rather live to work" are healthier, happier, and more productive. This philosophy is not only good for business, it's good for all of us.

THE "GOOD" MOTHER

I try to stay out of other people's squabbles, but I'm going to jump feet first into this one.

Let's get it out in the open—there's a cold war between the Office Moms and the Home Moms.

◄••►

Child Magazine says that neither group is trying very hard to understand the other, and that there are feelings of envy and resentment on both sides. Let's look at the results of a survey they conducted with two groups— "working" and "non-working" mothers. (Please excuse any unintentional judgments these labels contain. I use these labels only for the survey's sake.)

Forty-nine percent of the nonworking mothers said the employed mothers didn't spend enough time with their children.

The article didn't state how the employed mothers responded about the amount of time they spent with their children. (The working women I know would admit that sometimes they have enough time with their kids, and sometimes they don't.)

Fifty percent of the working mothers said they found their jobs stimulating.

Eighty percent of the nonworking mothers said they found a lot of things attractive about staying home. But, sixty-four percent said they would welcome the stimulation and sense of identity a job might offer.

Now it gets interesting.

Twenty-five percent of non-working mothers said they felt women in their group made better mothers. Only *two percent* of working mothers said they believed they were better mothers.

And, not surprisingly, working mothers expressed their unhappiness with the attitude of some stay-at-home mothers, who say mothers shouldn't work at all.

◀••▶

The July 11, 1998 *Los Angeles Times* reported a recent study conducted by the Kaiser Family Foundation, Harvard University and the *Washington Post*. Two thirds of those surveyed said that, financial needs aside, it is better if women can stay at home and care for their families. Half of those polled said they respect stay-at-home mothers more than those who work while their children are young. (63% of mothers of pre-schoolers are in the paid workforce.)

"Essentially, we found that people are living the life of Murphy Brown, but still hold the values of Ozzie and Harriet," said Kaiser Family Foundation President Drew Altman, contrasting the single working mom of TV's "Murphy Brown" sitcom with the married icons of the 1950s.

This is the problem as I see it: both groups are making judgments based on narrow ideas about the roles of women. And these judgments are being fueled by individual and collective dissatisfaction, and more than a little unresolved guilt and ambivalence.

This "mother-bashing" is hurtful and erodes our sense of community. How do we put an end to it?

Here's what I recommend:
1. Pair up with another mother. If you're a working mother, find a stay-at-home mom. If you're a stay-at-home, find a working mom.
2. Make a date to meet at one of your homes.
3. Sit down together. Coffee or tea is optional.
4. Tell her what you envy about her.

5. Tell her what's missing or unsatisfying in your life that leads to misunderstanding between you.
6. Tell her what you appreciate about her.
7. Now it's her turn to do #4, #5, and #6.
8. Say you're sorry for judging her so harshly.
9. Ask for her forgiveness.
10. Make up.
11. Go home.

We need to take more time to understand each other's unique situations. Some women feel they don't have a choice about whether to stay home or not. For some, going back to work is a triumph; for others, it's a grim necessity. Their family's financial situation influences, and in some cases, determines their decision.

The vast majority of mothers I meet have worked outside the home at some point in their lives. A great number of them worked less when the children were young and then gradually returned to a more full-time situation as they felt they and their children could handle it.

This demonstrates a conscious effort to be sensitive to the needs of their children, their family finances, and themselves.

Today, there is a resurgence of women who do not return to their jobs after they have had their babies. Some never work outside the home again. Financial freedom, or living on less to simplify their lives, seems to be the two motivating factors.

Of the women who return to the workforce, the majority pick up where they left off after their maternity ends. Many come back to new flex-time arrangements.

Those who wait until their children enter pre-school or elementary school usually do not find their old job waiting for them. They may look for a related job or pursue new directions or possibly, new careers. Or, like me, begin businesses of their own.

There is no one right way to be a good mother in our society. There are excellent ways to parent that have very little to do with time, and everything to do with the quality of the parent-child relationship, and the consistency of the love and guidance the parent provides.

Take my advice. Work on what's missing or unsatisfying in your life. That will leave little time for judging the lives of others. And, let's not set the standard for being a "good mother" so high that no woman can meet it.

Adventures In Gymnastics

I have had to miss more of my daughter's special events in the past few years than I ever predicted I would. My absenteeism stirs up all kinds of images that directly conflict with what I think a "good mother" is.

→

The time I almost missed her birthday party was the worst. I had scheduled an early flight home on a Sunday, with a plane change in Memphis. My scheduled arrival time was 12:30 PM, five hours before my daughter's birthday party was supposed to start. Everything was organized and ready to go.

Everything, that is, except the plane out of Memphis. The ticket agent announced it was going to be grounded for 5 HOURS because the mechanics had to replace a part that needed to be flown in—from Minneapolis!

I couldn't believe it. Not only might I be late for her party, I might miss it altogether! GOOD MOTHERS DON'T MISS THEIR CHILDREN'S BIRTHDAY PARTIES!

I stood in the airport terminal, crying over the phone to my husband, Alan. Tears of frustration and anger poured down my cheeks.

It took a few minutes to compose myself. I asked my husband not to tell our daughter about the delay, because I didn't want her to worry. We also agreed to tell her that I would be coming directly to the party at the roller rink instead of stopping at home first.

Then I called the car service that was to meet me in San Francisco. I spoke to my driver and explained the problem. I told him the party started at 6:00 PM, I wouldn't land until 5:30, and the roller rink was an hour from the airport. His reply was "No problem," which made me think he hadn't heard a word of what I said. He said he would look at his map for any possible shortcuts and meet me at baggage claim.

At exactly 5:30, we landed. I rushed off the plane, ran through the terminal, called my husband, and told him he was going to have to

→

supervise 22 eleven-year-olds until I got there. "Just smile and remember to breathe," I said. Then, I spotted my driver, who had grabbed my luggage off the carousel and was heading out the door with it. I hung up the phone and ran to catch up with him.

It was now 5:45. I had 15 minutes to make it to the party an hour away.

"Any ideas?" I asked, as I slid into the back seat.

"Well, not many people know this, but before I started my limo service, I was a professional race driver. If you want to get to your daughter's party fast, I can get you there."

When you're wracked with as much guilt as I was, risking your life seems like a small price to pay. "OK," I agreed. "But you'll have to let me split the speeding ticket, if we get one." I took a deep breath and tightened my seat belt.

As we sped through the streets of San Francisco, he asked me, "Have you ever seen any James Bond movies?" I couldn't remember. I was too focused on the speedometer. It read 85mph.

At 6:15 we arrived at the roller rink, 30 minutes ahead of schedule, and only 15 minutes late. The look on my daughter's face as I rushed in was one of joy and total forgiveness. We hugged each other tightly.

Luckily, I had arrived in one piece. In the future, for my sake, as well as my family's, I won't resort to such reckless behavior. (I won't have to. I'm boycotting a certain airline for making me almost miss my daughter's party.) ▲

FLEXIBILITY: *Don't Hurt Yourself!*

Before we go any further, I need to use two "F" words. Come on now, you know them as well as I do. You've said them a million times—*Flexibility* and *Forgiveness*.

And since you already know these words, let's be sure we're all clear on their meaning.

Look at the two conversations below. Which one demonstrates a *flexible* attitude and which one demonstrates an *inflexible* attitude?

Conversation #1:
"Give me the remote."

"No, you had it last night."

"Yeah, but at least we watched something socially responsible, not this garbage."

"Read a socially responsible book."

"No. You put on your headphones, so I don't have to hear this."

"I hate the headphones. I always get tangled up in the wires. I want to buy cordless ones."

"They cost too much."

"OK, then I'll just watch this for another 5 minutes, to see if Doug saves the boy."

"Then, turn down the volume."

"I can't hear if I do."

◄••►

"Then, switch channels so we can watch something we both enjoy."
"No way . . ."

Conversation #2:
"Give me the remote."
"No, you had it last night."
"Fine. Here! Just take it! Good night!"
"Honey?" (silence) "Honey . . .?" (More silence) "OK, we can
   watch your show."

If you thought that Conversation #2 demonstrated a flexible attitude, you're right . . . and notice how much more convenient it is if the *other* person is flexible!

Let's check the definition of our other "F" word, "forgiveness." Read the next two statements: all you have to do is correctly identify which statement illustrates *forgiveness* and which statement illustrates its opposite, *baloney*. Ready?

Statement #1
Jerry Springer, host of a talk show that glorifies physical and verbal abuse, was quoted as saying that "he knows his show is stupid, but it's OK to be stupid for one hour a day."

Statement #2
On the first day at her job, Susan mistakenly ran important documents through the paper shredder. Her supervisor didn't fire her.

If you identified Statement #1 as real baloney, then you are correct.

Forgiveness is about compassion; it's not a means to justify irresponsible behavior.

We are all gymnasts-in-training on this balance beam. And we're not going to last five minutes up here, if we don't learn how to be flexible and forgiving. Of course, you could always *try* to navigate up here without those qualities, but no gymnast in her right mind would perform without first limbering up. The risk of straining or pulling a muscle is too high.

And, the gymnast who won't pick herself up off the mat and try again, because she thinks she wasn't supposed to fall off in the first place, will never make progress. It takes forgiveness to allow herself the mistakes that come with learning.

The greatest obstacle for developing a healthy sense of flexibility and forgiveness is what I call the "Rules That Run You Ragged." You won't see these rules posted on a wall. They are self-imposed, often unconscious beliefs that force you to respond rigidly, as though you were on automatic pilot. Here's what's really scary: people operate by these rules *fifty to ninety percent* of the time!

You hear them in your head, like a broken record. Many of them are time-worn clichés like "Try Hard," "Be Strong," and "Be Nice." I have a cartoon on my office wall of a woman waiting for her bus. As she waits, here's what runs through her mind:

> *"Think positively, stop worrying, be myself, take a risk, be open with people, don't slouch, be more aggressive, start my diet . . . now I know there's something else I'm supposed to do today . . ."*

If you're operating by these relentless rules, when you're in a situation that calls for you to be resourceful and creative, you won't be able to do it. You'll end up feeling powerless and pushed into acting in ways that don't work for you.

We need to create some flexible, sane solutions for living. And, we start by rewriting some of the rules that run us ragged.

ADVENTURES IN GYMNASTICS

Come back with me to 1983. We are barreling down Highway 101 in my Toyota Tercel. It's a thirty-minute commute from my home to my office and I've left myself twenty minutes. (Been there, done that?)

As I'm speeding down the road passing everything in sight, out from under the hood comes what sounds like gremlins banging pots and pans together.

But, do I stop? No! Because I've got a client waiting for me and I CAN'T BE LATE! So, I *ignore* the billowing smoke coming out from under the hood and the frantic gestures of people passing me. And I'm thinking, "If I can just get to my exit, there's a garage at the bottom of the ramp. I can drop off the car, jog the rest of the way to work, and *still* meet my client on time!"

→

Somehow my car coughs, sputters, and rolls to a dead stop in the mechanic's driveway. But, *I'm elated*! I've got five minutes until my appointment and I'm only a four-minute sprint away! I toss the car keys to the mechanic and say: "I know it's nothing serious. I'll be back at 5:00 to pick it up."

I wish you could have seen the look on his face. (It had been a while since he'd seen someone *this* out of touch.) He walked over to my car, lifted the hood, looked under the hood, looked at me, shook his head, looked under the hood again, and let out a big sigh. "Lady, I don't know what you've been doing. But, somehow, you've managed to bake your battery, cook your carburetor, and your engine is a deep, toasty brown."

There is a beautiful gold frame on my wall, in my office. And in it is the bill . . . for $2800 . . . *for the new engine I had to buy for a two-year-old car.* Because I COULDN'T BE LATE.

If you had car trouble tomorrow, many of you would pull over and call your office to tell them you were going to be late. Or, you might use your car phone to relay the message. But, I'd bet that you'd just as likely push your car just a *little further*, so you wouldn't have to listen to that voice in your head shouting, "BE ON TIME!"

I can't afford to chalk up a lot of expensive lessons in my life. Neither can you. So, give this some thought: Are there any gremlins making knocks and pings under your hood? And if so, are you listening to them? Or, are you waiting until you see smoke? If you wait until then, I promise, it's going to cost you. ▲

◄••►

These rules are not all bad. They serve a purpose. At their best, they provide some social guidelines, like "Wait until everyone is seated before you start to eat." (We've got a ways to go on that one at our house.)

But, when they become the driving force behind our thoughts and actions, we are robbed. We can't even think what response will work best for us. We miss the signs. And we end up with frequent stressful episodes, escalating problems, and no one at the wheel.

For example, let's say you can't find your keys as you are leaving the house. Would you have the flexibility to think, "I'll look for them later," and take your back-up set instead? (Oh, you don't *have* a back up set? If your odds of never losing your keys are that good, call me and we'll go to Las Vegas.)

Or, do you operate by stress-producing rule #247, "I've Got to Find Those Keys!" and rush around tearing the place apart? And as you dash through the house, you not only trash the place, but a voice from inside your head trashes *you*! "I should have put them right back in my purse. Why didn't I put them by the front door?! I'm so stupid!"

I've got news for you. Trying to remember where you left your keys when you're in this state of mind is going to be very unproductive. Studies have shown that our mental ability drops by 25% when we're under this kind of stress. Translated, this means only *75% of you is looking for your keys*. No wonder you can't find them!

◀••▶

And, as you fly from room to room, you're also getting paranoid. If you live with roommates, you start to imagine that one of them took your keys. If you live alone, you think that a burglar stole them. And, if you have small children, you think someone tossed them down the heating duct. (That hunch, by the way, may be correct.)

So, now it becomes important to find the keys *and* to find out who took them. This gives your already over-stressed brain cells a real workout. Not until you stop, breathe and remember that *your keys are not a greatly coveted item* will your brain return to its normal state. Then you will simply look where you've already looked *three times*, and your keys will be there, as though by magic.

Let's look at two other rules that run women ragged—"Please Others First" and its close cousin, "Be Nice." In our society girls are raised to be "noticers." They are taught to notice other people's needs, and to accommodate them with a smile. When these girls grow into women, they try valiantly to take care of everything and everyone and find that either they can't deliver on their promises, or they work overtime to please everybody and never have time for themselves.

They focus too much on the feelings and needs of others and become unable to identify their own. Or worse yet, they develop a persona that's right out of the movie, *The Stepford Wives*—bland, pleasant and lethal.

As you might guess, this kind of self-detachment can lead to depression, substance abuse, over-eating, and all kinds of physical ailments.

◄••►

In my programs for people who give for a living—nurses, teachers, and counselors, for example—we do an exercise that helps them identify what they give, who they give to, and why.

We start by having participants spend a minute talking to the person next to them. Next, they write down as many words as they can that describe their neighbor, based on the conversation they just had. Then, in a column to the right of their first list, each person writes down all the words she can think of to describe herself.

Guess which list is longer? The one they made about the person they just met! And you know what happens next, when these people are asked to read a few of their best qualities to the group? There's nearly a stampede for the door! Because giving people are uncomfortable letting others know their strengths. They don't want to sound "boastful" or "too full of themselves."

And all of this discomfort over sharing qualities like "responsible" and "caring." (This doesn't happen with men. I did this exercise with a group of lawyers one morning, and they didn't finish reading their own lists until after noon.)

To help women tune in to and monitor their giving, I asked them the following questions:

1. What are you giving?
2. Why are you giving it?
3. How is giving it affecting you?

◄•••►

Then they fill in the blanks in these statements:

4. When I take time for myself I feel _____.
5. When I turn down a request for help from someone I feel

    _____.
6. The last time I gave something to myself was _____.

The most common answers are:

4. "guilty"
5. "guilty"
6. "can't recall"

If you are operating by the rules, "Be Nice" and "Please Others First," here are some tips:

- Practice saying "no" in advance of a situation where you might feel pressured to say "yes."
- Tell others directly what you want.
- Take time each day to think through your priorities and activities.
- Ask yourself: "What is it I need right now?" and answer it throughout the day. (Even if you don't have a clue in the beginning, after awhile, just getting into the habit of tuning in will help you find the answers you're looking for.)

REWRITING YOUR RULES

Staying loose and limber gives you the chance to think and act resourcefully in a challenging situation. You know the saying that "some rules are meant to be broken." Well, some rules are meant to be *rewritten*. So, start rewriting yours.

Instead of demanding too much from myself, I can _____
_____
_____.

Instead of focusing too much on others, I can _____
_____
_____.

Instead of trying too hard to please others, I can _____
_____
_____.

Now come up with some rules of your own to rewrite:

Instead of _____, I can _____
_____
_____.

Instead of _____, I can _____
_____
_____.

FLEXIBILITY: *An Exercise in Role Juggling*

A colleague of mine, who is involved with the work and family life movement and works zealously to change the way employers treat parents, recently confided to me that he had given up on the notion of balance. From now on he would use the word "blend" to describe the often competing responsibilities at work and at home.

I couldn't resist asking him if that meant we could look forward to seeing new jargon like "wamily," now that "work" and "family" would be blended. He looked at me. Then, without a word, he walked away. Zealots have no sense of humor.

OK, maybe I didn't give his idea a chance. So, that night I tried to imagine what would happen if we really did blend the very different parts of our lives together. Like what would happen, for example, if you blended sex and exercise together? Would you get "sexercise?"

Or, what if you are scheduled to present a report at an important meeting. You've also got to stop at the grocery store on your way home from work. So you decide to blend these two unrelated tasks together. Now, instead of reporting the company's quarterly profits, you read your co-workers your shopping list. And while you're waiting in line at the grocery store, you dazzle fellow shoppers with your projected revenue figures. Sorry. I just can't picture it.

◀••▶

Jonica Preitc, a mother and Silicon Valley employee who lives in Fremont, California, can't imagine blending her different tasks and activities either.

"For me, the secret to balancing work and family responsibilities is to keep them as separate as possible. During my workday, normally 7:30 a.m. to 5 p.m., I give 100 percent plus. I refrain from calling family and friends during the day. I save one lunch a week for doing banking, dry cleaning, etc. Usually once a quarter, I use a vacation day to get caught up on appointments and personal responsibilities that can't be done on weekends.

When I'm home, I concentrate on spending time with my family. That means keeping meals simple but making it a point to sit down and have dinner as a family. Bath time, stories, and a game usually follow dinner before bedtime.

Thursday night is family night which means going to watch my husband play softball and have pizza afterward. Finally, I keep my sanity by having my night out every Tuesday. That usually means an aerobics class and a soak in the spa."

This blending/balancing debate is not just a matter of semantics. The idea of blending different ingredients of our lives suggests that we'll end up with a smooth batter sooner or later. *This will never happen.* There will always be some lumps that won't disappear or some dry ingredients stuck at the bottom of the bowl, no matter how much stirring you do.

◄••►

Our lives have been called a juggling act—a more accurate description. Everyday we attempt to keep many balls in the air without getting hit in the head. And what makes this so complicated is that you and I know we're not really juggling balls. We're juggling car pools, errands, work deadlines, meetings, appointments, and a social life, just for starters.

Whenever I talk to women about role juggling, they are divided into three camps: those who *want to learn* all sorts of tips that could help them juggle their different demands, a second group that *doesn't want to hear* how the truly competent woman manages so well, and the third camp, which I believe is the largest, that *wants to learn that there are no truly competent women*, or at least no women who are managing any better than they are.

This fear of inadequacy keeps women from realizing their own wonderful competence.

To overcome this fear, we need to demonstrate to ourselves, once and for all, how well we juggle our multi-role lives. Try this therapeutic exercise at home, in your own kitchen.

ROLL JUGGLING EXERCISE

Here's what you'll need:

1. 18 dinner rolls—fresh or stale
2. 2 paper bags
3. 1 magic marker
4. Pad of writing paper and pen
5. 1 friend with a camera (with film in it)

On one bag write: "Roles I want to keep." On the other bag write "Roles to delegate, negotiate, or eliminate."

Now, stand up and stretch your arms out to your sides like an airplane at about shoulder height. Keep them steady.

Next, you will have one minute to come up with all the roles that you play in your life. Have your friend time you. And, for every role you name, your friend will place a dinner roll on your outstretched arms. Your job is to not laugh and keep your arms steady.

Here are some possible roles: Daughter, Wife, Mother, Volunteer, Homework Helper, Chauffeur, Employee, Cook, House Cleaner, Gardener, Lover (did you almost forget that one?), Bill Payer . . . See how easy it is? And remember, roles like Coupon Clipper count!

Once your sixty seconds are up, have your friend take your picture.

→

This is *definitely* a Kodak moment. While you've still got the rolls on your arms, tune in to what you're feeling and answer these questions.

1. **What's it like carrying so many roles?**
2. **Do you feel like it's a stretch?**
3. **Do you feel weighted down?**
4. **Would you just love to toss those rolls and feel the freedom of having NO responsibilities? THEN DO IT!!!**

Now pick up the rolls and put them on the kitchen table next to the two paper bags that you've labeled. Pick up a roll and assign it one of the roles you named a moment ago. Then place it in the bag of your choice. As you do that for each roll, have your friend write down which roles you want to keep and which ones you want to delegate, negotiate or eliminate.

When you've finished placing all the rolls in the bags, look at your list. What roles do you want to keep? Do you notice anything about them? Chances are you've chosen to keep the ones that give you satisfaction, stimulation, and fulfillment.

What about the rolls in the other bag? What do they have common? Most likely, they stand for the boring or routine tasks that you don't like to do.

And what about the tasks that involve taking care of others? Do

→

you have a lot of those? Of all the roles we play, these are the most depleting. These roles call for more support and help from others. Count how many of those roles you have and note which bag you placed them in.

Your last step is to review your list and, put the letter "D" by one role you want to delegate, the letter "N" by a role you want to negotiate, and the letter "E" by a role you want to eliminate. Don't worry if you can't figure out how you'll make these changes; we'll get to that a little later.

A Wellesley College study of the quality of women's life roles showed that women need be less concerned about the *quantity* of roles in their lives and more concerned about the *quality* of them. Here, we examine the quality and the weight of our roles to identify how helpful or hurtful they are. The nature and quality of a woman's various roles matters at least as much as their number. And there is a limit as to our energy and resources.

Do these multi-role lives we lead create stress? Yes, says *Working Mother* magazine. Seventy-nine percent of the women surveyed consider themselves more stressed than their mothers. And sixty-nine percent reported that they were happier.

How can that be? Because being busy seems to have its own interesting and complex rewards. The main cause of much of the increased stress had to with having more options and taking on diversified roles and responsibilities, both at work and home.

When busy women are asked to describe the benefits derived by leading sometimes hectic, multi-role lives, they use words like a "sense of accomplishment or fulfillment" or a "sense of purpose and satisfaction."

Nancy Snyderman, author of *Dr. Nancy Snyderman's Guide to Good Health: What Every Forty-Plus Woman Should Know About Her Changing Body*, cites an incident in high school where someone else told her how many roles she could handle.

> *"I was called into the dean of students' office when I was going into my senior year. And the dean said, 'You have to drop one of your extracurricular activities.' I asked why. She said, 'You're taking on too much.' 'Are my grades suffering?' I asked. She said, 'No. But it just looks like you have too much.'"*

> *"So I was given a choice between cheerleading and being the editor of the yearbook. I dropped cheerleading. And I think I never got over it, that someone else would look at my life and say, 'We've decided from the outside that this is too much for you.'"*

Research has consistently shown that the more roles a woman occupies, the better her mental and physical health. A 1991 book called *Juggling*, by Faye J. Croby, discussed the benefits and struggles of dealing with a life with so many parts. The thinking then was, and is now, that taking on many life roles—worker, mother, wife, daughter, friend—can act as a buffer against the blues, by providing more avenues of self-expression, just as it always has for men.

Dr. Snyderman says in her book, "I like the option of saying yes or no, and I think the more diversified my life, the happier I am. And so far, because I'm a reasonably good list-maker and organizer, I've been able to juggle things."

Rebekah Mulder, a 55-year old real-estate agent in Santa Barbara, says she balances her job with her husband, children, and grandchildren and is active in her church and in a civic group. "Everything I do I really love," she says.

While working mothers may rate their stress high, they are just as likely to work best with a lot on their plate. They feel stimulated and enriched. And, when they don't give in to a culturally sanctioned sense of guilt, they are filled with excitement and self-esteem. The jugglers find a great deal of pleasure in life—more than women with few life roles.

When a woman's roles are limited or when the quality of her roles is poor, she is less happy. Here is one woman's fantasy about what would happen if she gave up the caretaking and mundane roles in her life:

"The babysitter would be a combination of Mister Rogers and Mary Poppins. A housekeeper would do the mundane pain-in-the-ass cleaning and cooking and shopping; a secretary would take care of the bills and answering the phone. And, I'd go out and work!"

She also felt that with this arrangement, she would delight in being with people, would have a great sense of humor, and would be more creative.

◀••▶

There's a very real chance that you can arrange your life to *have* these qualities instead of just *imagining* them. What it would take is the willingness and know-how to let go of the roles that you don't want to perform, and support for the roles that you must.

Eight-five percent of Americans in one recent survey say they are happy. And, what these people said kept them happy day in and out were the little things—a loving family, interesting work, loyal friends—not the tasks they felt were outside of their priorities.

Another source of unhappiness for women is when their roles conflict to an extreme. One woman said she was contending with her husband's bad health, her pregnancy with a second child, her parents' divorce, her still-wobbly law practice, and her worries about finances. Any one of these by itself would be emotionally and time-consuming. Together, they can seem overwhelming.

And how do you measure "overwhelming?" One way is to assign values to your daily responsibilities and different life events.

For example, using the Stress Test developed by Holme and Rahe, divorce would score 75 points (high), on-the-job trouble, 30 (medium) and your child needing glasses, 15 (low).

Check your own levels on some of these common stressors:

Divorce..75, Death..65, Birth of baby..50, Moving..50,
Money problems..40, Single parenthood..40, Two career couple..30,
Finding or changing day care..20, You do most of the housework..13,
Change in diet or exercise..10, Work schedule changes..10

◀ •• ▶

The Stress Test lists over 50 stress items to score. If your total score is over 200, that means you are under an inordinate amount of pressure and need to talk to a therapist, shed extra commitments, and enlist support from friends.

If your score between 135-199, you're at a stage where things are particularly hectic. You may feel uncomfortably stretched and need extra help for awhile.

A score of 75-134 means that you are juggling wildly. Despite your crazed schedule, a little more quiet time is all you would need to realign your balance.

And I don't know anybody with a score under 74, so we'll skip that one.

It's humanly impossible to pay attention to all aspects of your work and family life at once. One week, your work might require a great deal of attention. Another week, a family crisis might override your work priorities. There are moments when you ought to invest emotionally in many different roles, and other moments when you may need to conserve your psychological energies.

Working Mother magazine reports that most women feel enriched, besides stressed, by juggling occupational and domestic responsibilities. Evidence shows that working-class women, as well as affluent women, enjoy working outside the home. They derive a sense of satisfaction and self-esteem from paid labor and dislike housework.

The demands of a complex multi-role life don't seem to have dampened working mothers' spirits. Despite the escalating pressure of the workplace, they are resilient and determined to succeed. Surprisingly, only 11% said they would never work again, even if they won the lottery!

While good mental health is not automatically assured by multiple life roles—certainly a bad marriage and a miserable job can cause depression—involvement in many roles seems to increase a woman's satisfaction with each one. The key is to end up living a multi-role life filled with roles that have meaning and value to you.

FLEXIBILITY: *Loosen Up—That's Where The Fun Is!*

As I sat down to write this chapter, I looked high and low for a story that I had planned to share with you. I had written it on a piece of paper. But now, the paper was gone.

Our rabbit had eaten it. All that was left was a paper clip, and a tiny scrap of paper covered with teeth marks.

Now, you might think, "What's a bunny doing in her office?" It's simple. She sits at my feet while I write. Because of my family's allergies, we can't have a dog. So I've taught our rabbit to behave like one.

She makes a wonderful companion, until I turn my back. Then, she'll eat anything made of wood, including important pieces of paper that have fallen on the floor.

When I discovered the story I was planning to use had become bunny food, I paused to consider my options. I could:

1. Serve rabbit stew for dinner.
2. Rant and rave.
3. Say terrible things about myself to myself.
4. Try to re-construct the story from memory.
5. Stay flexible and forgiving.

I chose the fifth option. Funny thing, the moment I did, my brain began to humor me. I started thinking about those kids who try to get out of doing their homework by telling the teacher that "the dog ate it."

Even though I graduated from elementary school some time ago, suddenly I was back in 4th grade again, feeling cornered to come up with a good excuse *fast*.

Then, as quickly as the flashback started, it ended, taking my anxiety with it. And, what amazed me was that I didn't get bent of shape about losing that story. I just started writing again.

Which brings us to our next point about flexibility. Up here on the balance beam, you can't afford to get bent out of shape. If you get into a cramped position, you'll surely lose your footing and fall. We gymnasts need to keep ourselves loose and flexible, so that we can perform fluidly in times of stress.

When you combine flexibility and forgiveness, not only will you be more productive, you'll have a whole lot more fun.

On a flight to Houston recently, I had the opportunity to test this theory. A flight attendant had just delivered my meal, low fat, of course. In the tray was an herbal tea bag.

"I'd like some hot water for my tea, please," I said, as she came down the aisle with her beverage cart.

"We don't have any," she replied.

"You must have some," I insisted. "You gave me this tea bag."

◀••▶

"We don't have any," she said again.

"That's ridiculous," I argued. "You must have hot water for your tea drinkers, especially since the tea was your idea in the first place!"

"We don't have any," she repeated.

My heart began to pound, my neck muscles tensed into tight cords, and my face turned bright red. I knew I was dangerously close to having an attack of what the in-flight magazine called "Air Rage." That's when passengers feel hassled or powerless and become verbally—and sometimes physically—explosive. Sounded good to me.

Should I risk getting arrested for mowing down a flight attendant with her beverage cart? Or, should I loosen up and have some fun? It was a tough choice.

I smiled sweetly at her and said, "No hot water? No problem. I'll just wad up this tea and chew it like tobacco. You don't mind if I spit it here in the aisle, do you?"

She nearly tripped running to the galley to fetch some hot water. And I just laughed and laughed.

When you allow yourself an extra few seconds to stand back and see the absurdity in a situation, the possibilities of enjoying yourself—and solving your problems—are endless.

ADVENTURES IN GYMNASTICS

Granted, sometimes you have to dig deep to find that reservoir of flexibility and forgiveness. A client of mine in Raleigh, North Carolina, discovered this a few months ago. She had just returned home from shopping with her two children, ages two and four. The phone rang and she took the call, leaving the grocery bags and the children alone in the family room.

When she got off the phone a few minutes later, she found the four-year-old with an open bottle of chocolate syrup in her hand. Her daughter had decorated the entire room—the white sofa, the white chairs, the white table, and the white carpet—with chocolate syrup. It looked like the world's largest ice cream sundae. All she needed was some nuts, a cherry, and a little whipped cream.

When she answered my call a few moments later, she was hyperventilating. "I can't believe this! There's chocolate syrup everywhere! And, in two hours our realtor is bringing over a couple to look at the house!!"

I had called to talk business. Instead, my crisis intervention skills kicked in. "Listen carefully," I said. "There are two things you need to do. First, take some deep breaths." She did. "Now, go get your camera and a phone book."

"All right," she said. "But, don't go away. I'm considering child abuse."

→

◄•••►

"I'm right here," I assured her. "Go get those things and come right back to the phone. And stay away from the family room."

A minute later she was on the phone again. "OK, now what?" she asked.

"Open the Yellow Pages and find a carpet cleaner that does emergency work," I said. "They might offer services for water damage, problems like that," I added.

She scanned the pages silently. "Got one," she said.

"Good. When we get off the phone, call them. But, before you do that, you need to do one more thing. It may sound wacky, but just trust me. Take your camera into the family room. Get the kids' attention, and tell them you want to take their picture. Just before you snap the shot, tell them to smile and say, 'Look, Mom, just like Martha Stewart!' "

"You've got to be kidding. I'm ready to kill them," she said.

"I know," I replied. "Do it anyway."

"OK, but only because you're an expert."

"Thanks. I'll wait for you."

I held my breath and listened closely. Then came the sound I had been hoping for—laughter. Gales of it.

She picked up the phone, still laughing. "I can't believe it! My family room's a disaster and I'm laughing!"

I said, "Congratulations! And, best of all, your kids are still alive!"

There's a happy ending to this decorating disaster. My client sold her house that evening. And she has decided not to decorate their new home all in white. →

◄•••►

Flexibility and forgiveness don't always appear when we need them. But, with a little laughter, they are likely to show up sooner. And when something awful happens, don't say, "You know, years from now, we'll look back at this and laugh." START LAUGHING NOW!! ▲

LOOSE AND LIMBER SOLUTIONS FROM OTHER GYMNASTS

From Janet Konttinen: "It was a big accomplishment when my son graduated from diapers. And he wanted everybody to recognize his achievement. But unlike mastering the bicycle, tying shoes, or climbing to the top of the magazine rack at Safeway, people may not always notice. So he solved this problem by wearing his new Batman underpants over his trousers. He is very popular."

From Harriet Lerner, Ph.D., author of *The Dance of Deception*: "I've developed a theory of 'rotating neglect.' I rotate what I neglect so that no one thing—work, kids, spouse, friend—is overlooked for long."

From Linda, single mother of a teen-age daughter: "I gave up vacuuming cold turkey. Now I use that time to spend with my daughter. About every three months, when the dust bunnies get too thick, we call in a cleaning service."

From Jane Condon, stand-up comic, mother of two boys: "I want to be a good mother, I really do. The kind who gets the clothes out of the dryer and folds them while they're still warm. I'm lucky if I get them out while they're still in style."

◀••▶

From Beth Lindsmith: "Loose button? Use duct tape."

From Suyin Stein: "I just hired a cleaning person. I've never used one before, and I wasn't exactly ready. So, we're starting out slow. I tell her, 'Give me two sparkling bathrooms. As we unclutter, you can clean the rest of the rooms.'"

Ellen Galinsky, Co-founder of the Family and Work Institute: "Don't insist on quality time with your children. It's during the loose unstructured time when parents and kids simply hang out together—in the back yard, in the kitchen, running errands—that kids bring up the 'little pains of the day' and real parent-child closeness ensues."

SOCKS THAT SPLIT UP AND THE WOMEN (AND MEN) WHO MATCH THEM

Over the years, I've met an extraordinary number of intelligent people who don't get the joke about socks: *No matter what you do, there will always be odd socks.* Instead, they valiantly try to create total order where none can exist.

Here are some real-life solutions that otherwise normal people have come up with:

One of my friends sent her daughter, Kate, to a Halloween party dressed as the "Odd Sock Fairy." Kate's business card read *Collecting your odd socks since 1987!* You might think this was a cute, innocent costume. But, I happen to know that my friend secretly hoped her daughter would

◄••►

bring home socks that would match the odd ones she had been saving for *two years*!

William, father of twin girls, has the responsibility of dressing them each morning. He came up with this unique system; he writes large numbers on the soles of each sock in permanent ink, so they will be easy to match.

I wondered why he did this, in light of the fact that the girls' socks are white, the same size and interchangeable.

"I want each girl to each have her own socks, especially because they are twins," he answered.

"OK," I said. "But how does that explain the numbers on *your* socks?"

Then there are the people who safety-pin their socks together before they put them in the washer. Or they buy a product called Sock Savers® that keep the socks together. (You know who you are and there's nothing to be ashamed of.)

That leaves the rest of us. Are we just reckless fools, throwing our socks into the washer together, naively believing that they will emerge from the dryer as a pair? Don't we realize that one of the socks could abandon the other at any point during the rinse and spin cycle?!

And what about when the socks tumble against each other in the soft warmth of the fluff cycle? The attraction in there is electric! What makes us think every sock will stick with its mate?

◀•••▶

Socks are just like some couples you may know. The pair seems well-matched in the beginning, they go through different cycles together, and then suddenly, for some unknown reason, they split up!

I used to believe that little piles of neatly color-coded socks would get me into heaven. Now I don't. Every weekend I sort seven pairs of socks for each person in my family, one pair for each day of the coming week. Then you know what I do with the rest of those multi-colored socks...? *I stand back and let them mingle in an atmosphere of cultural diversity.*

Sure, we have serious problems in our lives at times. But it's the small ones that drive us nuts. Look for the humor and absurdity in the petty annoyances and day-to-day problems you encounter. Then you'll be able to move through them with agility and style. And if your friends and family are telling you to "Loosen up!" because you react to each minor aggravation as though it were a national disaster, take their advice.

There's good and bad stress, and some of it is unavoidable. But getting *distressed* is usually your choice, one that you can manage by keeping your thoughts and actions loose and limber.

FLEXIBILITY: *Doing the Splits*

Sandra, Community Relations Director in a large health care system, told me a troubling, but all-too-common, story. On a Friday afternoon last January, she saw a whole department disappear, only to watch it creep into her job description the following Monday.

Since then, she's had to split her time between the work the old department left behind and her already established duties. "When I returned from a one-day conference recently, there were 19 messages on my voice mail and 23 on my E-mail!" she complained. "These days, I feel lucky when I can return messages within two weeks of receiving them!"

Sheryl, a single mother with two young children, lives near her ailing mother who needs daily assistance. The daughter splits her time between taking care of two households and working at a part-time job. "When I'm not at my paying job, I'm at my mother's," she said. "Plus, I run errands for her, shop for both of us, and have the girls with me three days a week."

Elizabeth, a stay-at-home mom with three children divides her time among "a hundred different things." She complains that most days she'll get a good start on a project, only to get sidetracked by the kids. During their nap times, she tries to pick up where she left off. And, if that doesn't work, she stays up late to finish, often doing housework and laundry after everyone's in bed.

◄••►

Do these women sound like anyone you know? Do you constantly split your time between tasks and people and frequently feel stretched to the limit?

When asked to consider their greatest source of job stress, 61% respondents in a 1996 study picked an increased work load. There is enormous pressure to do multiple tasks well, and increasing expectations that we can split our energies between two (or more) high-priority tasks.

My colleague is one of thousands of women who have been expected to absorb someone else's job description and do more with fewer resources. With so much work to shoulder, it's no wonder that 45% of the women reported feeling stressed out once a week and 38% three times a week.

Women who care for both a parent and have children at home must be particularly careful about over-extending themselves. Without the right support and the ability to farm out low priority tasks, they are prime candidates for depression, isolation, and job burnout.

And mothers with young children, who aim for a level of productivity that would require an additional eight hours a day, are bound to suffer muscle strain. No one can do the splits that long without serious consequences to their well-being.

The next time you see a gymnast perform the splits on the balance beam, watch her carefully. Even if she is competing in the Olympics, the look on the her face is one of total concentration. Why is that? Because **if you do the splits wrong, you can injure yourself.**

There is a right way to do the splits and a wrong way. The wrong way hurts . . . A LOT. You can hyper-extend your joints and muscles and end up writhing on the ground in pain. The right way allows you to extend yourself to your comfortable limits. It's a learned technique that must be performed *consistently*, but not *constantly*. Otherwise, you're inviting disaster.

Adventures In Gymnastics

One evening, my friend, Barbara, decided to cook a romantic dinner for her husband, Bob. She stopped work a little early and came upstairs from her office. As she gathered the ingredients for her special marinara sauce, her mood lightened; thoughts of her hectic day faded away.

She turned on her favorite CD and poured herself a glass of red wine. She sipped it slowly, savoring its taste. As her thoughts drifted to pleasure-filled fantasies of the night ahead, her hips began to sway to the music. The marinara sauce bubbled in the pot, its aroma arousing her senses.

A few minutes later Barbara heard the familiar sound of the fax machine. She fought the urge to retrieve the fax, but gave in when she remembered she hadn't heard back from an important client. So, she went downstairs to read her client's message, taking her wine with her.

$\rightarrow$

Unfortunately, he needed to discuss an urgent matter. So, she set the glass of wine on her desk and dialed his number. No sooner had she gotten him on the line, when she swung around in her chair and knocked the glass over. Instantly, a stream of Cabernet spilled onto her cream-colored carpet.

Grabbing a box of tissues nearby, Barbara got down on the floor and blotted up what she could. Using one hand for cleaning, and the other to hold the phone against her ear, she valiantly kept up her end of the conversation, while her client—oblivious to the crisis—continued to talk.

Five minutes later they finished. Fearing it was already too late, she raced upstairs for some salt. (She'd heard it lifted red wine stains from carpeting.)

And there, bubbling over the pot, onto the stove and the floor was the sauce she had forgotten. In one motion, Barbara grabbed the pot, dropped it in the sink, turned off the burner, and leaped over the river of marinara to get to the pantry. She yanked a box of salt off the shelf and raced downstairs.

The stain on the carpet had spread. She poured salt on it. The stain turned pink. Then Barbara remembered another remedy for wine stains—club soda. She frantically searched for a bottle. The moment she poured it over the salt, she knew she had made a mistake. Now, it looked like pink snow was melting under her desk.

With no solution in sight and feeling defeated, she gave up and trudged up the stairs to the kitchen, dreading what awaited her there.

◀••▶

Tomatoes, onions, mushrooms and green peppers stuck to the stove top and counter. Sauce had seeped under the stove. It took fifteen minutes to clean off the first layer, and she wasn't finished yet. There was more sauce on her blouse than there was left in the pot.

She didn't feel like swaying to the music anymore. She got a beer out of the refrigerator and banged a pot of water onto the stove for the pasta. Then she turned to the sink to try to salvage some remains of the sauce for dinner.

At that moment, Bob walked in, came up from behind and gave her a hug. "Smells good," he said. "What's for dinner?"

He immediately regretted those words . . . when she turned around.

Barbara and Bob ate at an expensive Italian restaurant that night. They were a few minutes late for their 7:30 dinner reservation, because Bob hadn't anticipated that it would take three shampoos to get the onions and tomatoes out of his hair. ▲

The key to not overextending yourself is to define what "fully extended" means *for you*. This means your version of the splits may look very different than someone else's. The woman in the previous story is a former aerobics instructor. Running up and down the stairs she could handle. Standing still, doing one thing at a time, was harder.

Another woman I know gives new meaning to the term "multi-task." Two years ago she moved to the country with her husband and children to seek a more serene life. Last week she called to catch up.

"What's that noise in the background?" I asked.

"Chickens. I'm feeding the chickens while we talk," she said.

"How do you manage that?" I asked.

"I got a cordless headset so that I can call my friends while I'm working," she explained.

"How's it working out?" I asked, intrigued.

"Great!" she told me. "Right now, I'm talking to you, feeding the chickens, supervising the workers in the apple orchard, and watching the kids on the play set."

"Well, you've certainly slowed down since you left the city," I remarked. "Got any bread baking in the oven?

"No . . . croissants." she replied.

When she's like this, she's a marvel to watch. She's loose and fluid, and clearly in her element. But, she also gets over-extended. When she calls me during one of those phases, the conversation is very different.

The last time we talked, her house guests had just left. After a week of over-extending herself to people who "didn't reciprocate or show any kind of gratitude," she was angry and resentful. While having house guests goes with her highly social nature, so does extending her already generous limits to the point of exhaustion.

For an entire week she had catered to people she barely knew, while her husband was out of town on business and she was in charge . . . of *everything*. If you don't adjust what "everything" means when you're under the kind of social siege she described, you're going to get burned.

She had been reluctant to ask her house guests to "do their share." (Knowing her, I bet that was something major like asking them to turn off the water after they brush their teeth.)

I, too, have gone through stretches like that—particularly during the holidays—when my time is devoted almost entirely to others, and the pace is non-stop. I get stretched beyond my limits and ending up paying for it.

If you don't recognize when to stop, and then *stop*, you could end up feeling angry, exhausted, and miserable. Or, you might end up calling a friend after a week of unwanted house guests and say, "I'm sitting here sipping on a Scotch I should have had the day they arrived."

HOW TO DO THE SPLITS WITHOUT HURTING YOURSELF:

1. Warm up. This is going to be quite a stretch.
2. Be sure the padded floor mats are in place, just in case you fall off the balance beam. You don't want to suffer a "stress fracture."
3. Fight the urge to show everyone that you can do the splits. Save it for when it really counts.
4. Monitor yourself so you'll know when you're moving out of your range of comfort.

5. Extend yourself slowly; remember, you can stop at any time.
6. Once you're fully extended, stop. There's nothing else you need to do, no matter what you think.
7. Don't let anyone else's version of the splits push you beyond what you can do. What is a comfortable extension for them may mean crutches for you.
8. If you're stretched to the max and can't get up, ask for help.

THE FINAL STRETCH

The key to being able to approach problems flexibly is to stay loose and limber. If you don't, you'll resort to rigid ways of thinking and acting that will create new problems for you. Holding on to and operating by rigid rules can keep you from experiencing your own special traits and strengths.

Rewrite the rules that dictate how you "should" or "ought" to act. Ask yourself: "Are the rules and principles prescribed by my role models and society good for me now, or are they unrealistic and outdated?"

The fastest way to access flexible thinking is through forgiveness. And once you find forgiveness, laughter is not far behind. As the stories in this section illustrated, when you can see the humor in a stressful situation, you're bound to end up with a unique solution for dealing with it.

Recognize that life makes demands on you; not all of them are reasonable. Being flexible doesn't mean you should stretch to accommodate everything and everybody. It means knowing what your comfortable limits are and staying flexible within them.

STRENGTH

Developing Muscle Tone

STRENGTH: *You Are a Gift—No Returns or Exchanges*

If you had to answer the question, "Who am I?" what would you say? Most people identify themselves as what they are—an employee, a parent, a jogger, a choir member. Few people think about who they are in terms of their unique human qualities that have nothing to do with their job, status or position.

In defining who you are, it helps to recognize your needs as a human being. Then you can commit to spending time, money, energy and effort to meet those needs. But, don't confuse what you *want* with what you *need*.

"What do I want?" repeated often enough, will produce within us jealousy, envy, insecurity, and perhaps bitterness and even narcissism. "What do I need?" is a better question and tougher one. It leads to self-esteem, well-being, and balance.

Ten important needs for every human being:

1. **Self-esteem:** do you recognize and accept your own value and worth?

2. **Humor:** do you look for and find the lighter side of stressful situations?

3. **Physical well-being:** are you practicing a healthy diet and getting good nutrition and exercise?

4. **Self-discipline:** do you have goals and objectives and follow a plan to achieve them?

5. **Positive attitude:** are you solution-oriented rather than problem-oriented?

6. **Productivity:** do you feel a sense of meaningful accomplishment and satisfaction from your endeavors?

7. **Appreciation of beauty:** do you take time to enjoy all that is beautiful in the world?

8. **Spiritual dimension:** do you feel connected to a power greater than yourself to achieve added meaning and purpose in your life?

9. **Healthy relationships:** do you interact positively with other people with an ability to care and empathize?

10. **Love:** do you express the value of yourself and others?

If you read this list and thought, "Oh, great. Look at all the things I'm not doing," then you've missed the point. These ten needs are *lifelong guidelines,* not items to be checked off a to-do list each day.

Honoring your needs as a human being will give you the strength to cope with the world. So, let's do a strengthening exercise. It's easy and it only takes two minutes each morning.

<···>

THE BOW EXERCISE

Step 1. Buy a bag of bows that you use to decorate gift packages. Choose any colors and sizes you like.

Step 2. Each morning, when you get out of bed, take a bow out of the bag; remove the adhesive back.

Step 3. Stand in front of the mirror . . . butt-naked.

Step 4. Stick the bow on your body, anywhere you like.

Step 5. Look in the mirror and repeat in a loud, affirming voice:

I am a gift. I am a gift to those who count on me each day. I am a gift to those who love me. And, most importantly, I am a gift to myself and will treat myself accordingly.

I didn't design this exercise just because it would be fun for us to get naked and decorate ourselves with bows. I did it for those mornings when we plunge into our lives without so much as a "good morning" to ourselves. And, if I could get you to stand in front of the bathroom mirror with just a bow on, I would get your attention.

Standing naked in front of the mirror can be a painful experience. Some of us have a regular ritual where we look to see what's holding up and what's falling down. Glumly watching gravity have its way with us, we consider our options—exercise, hot fudge sundaes, or plastic surgery.

Even Barbie, the world's best-selling toy, is set to undergo major plastic surgery on her body, her first in 20 years, according to the November 17, 1997 edition of the *Wall Street Journal*. At the ripe old age of 38, an age at which mortal flesh starts to sag, she will get a wider waist (hooray!), slimmer hips and a reduction of her legendary bust line.

According to Jean McKenzie, who heads Mattel Inc.'s Barbie division: "Her profile will be less graduated." (So those measurements of 38-18-34 weren't so realistic after all! And all along, I thought it was just me!)

Tomorrow morning, stand in front of the mirror and say, "I'm a gift."

"Impossible!" you say. "Silly!" you think. Just one more of those hokey affirmations. I'm dead serious. If you think of yourself as a gift, you're going to start *treating* yourself like one. And think about it. Do you throw gifts around, letting them get banged up or broken? No! You treat them with loving care, just as you would a treasured keepsake.

Women (and men) get trapped into thinking their sense of worth depends on how much they get done each day. The manager, who completes a big project at work on time, even though she's been out three days with the flu. The mother with three young children, who volunteers her time *and* works forty hours a week.

We get pulled into equating our value with what we *do* rather than who we are and confuse being a worthwhile person with our productivity. We admire the people who achieve the most in a given day. And sometimes, we elevate their accomplishments to the point where we think they are better than us. They may be more productive, yes. But, *better*? No!

Is it reasonable to think of yourself as a good person on the days you're on top of things, and a worthless wreck on the days you're not? Just because the computer crashes, you got a flat tire, and you're in danger of missing a major deadline, it doesn't mean your value as a human being has dropped...except perhaps, in your own mind.

OK, maybe you're not as *lovable* under acute stress as you are at other times. (My husband has made this comment to me once or twice during our marriage.) But, *your worth as a person is not open to negotiation.*

Tomorrow morning—no matter how much you got done the day before, no matter what the scale says—go to the mirror and put on your bow. If you know it's going to be an especially tough day, stick on *two* bows instead of one.

And, if you want a constant reminder throughout the day, wear your bow on your clothing. Display it proudly on your lapel. And when people ask you, "Why are you wearing a bow?" smile and say, "I'm a gift."

They won't laugh. They'll look at you in wonder and amazement. And, they'll wish they had a bow, too.

STRENGTH: *Does Guilt Get In Your Way?*

Not all guilt is equal. Ideally, guilt should function as the emotion that keeps us acting morally, ethically and honestly. But, all too often, we use it to punish ourselves for a crime we haven't committed.

For example, don't you hate it when you go to someone's home and they say, "Excuse the mess," and you spend the rest of your visit trying to find it? Your friend feels guilty about some undetectable flaw in her house-keeping, so she makes a big deal of it. And being a polite guest, you want to assure her that there's nothing to apologize for, until you realize there really *is* nothing to apologize for!

Now you're determined to find something messy somewhere, *any-where*. You scan the living room slyly. Every time she blinks, your eyes dart to a corner or a table. Nothing. Maybe the mess is in another room. So, you make an excuse to go into the kitchen. It's so clean, open-heart surgery could be performed on the floor.

You're thinking, "If *this* house is a mess, then what do *I* live in?!" You were feeling secure when you arrived. But, you're leaving with a case of con-tagious, unjustified guilt.

False guilt plays havoc with your emotions and makes you grovel, even when groveling is not called for. (Is groveling *ever* called for?) False guilt gets in the way and blocks your ability to move beyond emotions like embar-rassment. And the biggest culprit of all is three words: "I should have . . ."

◄•••►

And what exactly is it you *should* have done? Said "yes?" Said "no?" Been there? Done something? Said something? Oh, so many missed opportunities just waiting for us to agonize over! How will we ever fit them all in?

"Women working outside the home are prone to magical 'if-only' thinking," says author Jo Ann Larsen, author of *I'm a Day Late and a Dollar Short . . . and It's Okay!* (Deseret Book Company). "They tell themselves that if only they didn't work, if they just tended to their family twenty-four hours a day, they would never feel stressed out, their children would never get sick and everyone would always be happy," Larsen said in an interview in *Working Mother* magazine.

This kind of thinking reflects one of the major causes of guilt: impossible expectations. When you can't meet them, you feel guilty. It's that simple.

Take a Sunday last spring, for instance. My sister was visiting from Chicago, something she rarely did. Even though I had a busy speaking schedule, I wanted to be gracious. So I invited my parents and my sister for brunch.

I needed about eight hours to prepare for a four-day business trip and a speech I was scheduled to give on Monday. So, I told everyone in advance, "Once we're done eating, I will have to excuse myself." I explained my early departure to each person, so there would be no room for misunderstanding.

When the meal was over, I cleared some plates. Then, I went over to my sister to say good-bye.

She said, "You're going to leave now?! But, we didn't get any time to talk!" The effect of that gesture took me by surprise, like an avalanche that you don't see coming

My husband "suddenly" realized I was leaving for four days, and requested some time for just the two of us. It would, have been possible—and enjoyable—on Saturday, but not today.

My daughter, who needed to make some car pool arrangements and did it regularly, acted like she had never used the phone before. She needed my help.

And my father, who is quite frail and needs help getting around, suddenly had to go to the bathroom.

After my family's remarkable display of disappointment and dependency, I gave in and stayed another hour-and-a-half to send the message that I would really rather be with them. All the while, disturbing visions of standing in front of 300 people without anything to say kept popping into my head.

Finally, I announced that I really had to go. And that's when my mother delivered a line that shall forever remain in my treasure chest of guilt inducers. As she hugged me good-bye she said, "It's all right. We forgive you."

So, when I got to my office, did I sit down and work on my speech? No! I wrote this instead, to get the guilt *out* of my *head* and *into* my *computer*. Of course, when I finished I had *one less hour* to prepare for my speech and my trip. So far, guilt had cost me two-and-a-half hours of precious time.

Too bad it was a Sunday. Had it been a weekday, I would have called my insurance agent to ask if he had a policy that would protect me against all kinds of unwarranted pangs of guilt. And if he had said yes, I would have made his day. Because I was ready to buy guilt insurance and didn't care what it cost. "Just write it up, John. I'll get my checkbook."

There are so many things you can feel guilty about. Here are just a few:

1. Your housekeeping
2. Your kids
3. Your career
4. Your body
5. Lack of exercise
6. Being single
7. Being a single *parent*
8. *Not* being a parent
9. The "super moms"
10. Your old friends
11. Your closets
12. Your checking account

If we allowed ourselves to feel guilty for about half the items on this list—plus all the other things we let get to us—we wouldn't have time for anything else!

Is there a way out of this mire of guilt and self-flagellation?

◄••►

CURES FOR GUILT

Joan Borysenko, Ph.D., a psychologist and author of *Guilt is the Teacher, Love is the Lesson* (Warner Books), notes that unrealistic expectations are at the root of many guilty feelings. "Women set themselves up as having to be everything to everybody, and then paint the house at the same time. When they fail, they blame themselves. Once women set their sights more realistically, guilt subsides."

According to a study by *Working Mother* magazine, one in five working mothers professes to feel nearly guilt-free. These women have five special blessings—both psychological and social. Those who work by choice feel more satisfied about all aspects of life. The not-guilty working mothers also have: cooperative husbands, sympathetic employers, good child care and jobs that make it all worthwhile.

Even without all these blessings, it is still possible to reduce the number and severity of your guilt attacks. Here are some things to remember and practice:

- If you work, consider how your job benefits your family.
- Look for little ways to ease your guilt; sometimes a ten-minute cuddle with your kid before you start the day will do wonders for both of you.
- Change your self-talk; focus on what's going right.
- Set a time limit on your guilt; two minutes seems about right.
- Don't confuse guilt with anger and frustration; if there's a problem, resolve it rather than turn it inward.

- Look for better systems to manage your responsibilities.
- When you feel a guilt attack coming on, think about the choices you've made and whether you'd do things differently if you could. If you are secure and confident, it's easier to dismiss the flak you get from relatives, "friends," other parents, and total strangers.
- And, next time you're at the grocery store, keep an eye out for a product called GUILT BE GONE. They say one spray and guilt can be wiped away as easily as grime off a window. If you find it, let me know. I'll buy a case of it.

In the 1960's, psychoanalyst D.W. Winnicott began using a helpful phrase: the "good enough mother." What a relief this was from the "good mother" ideas that produced guilt in women who couldn't meet its impossible standards of self-sacrifice.

Try this term on for size: *Good enough*. It's roomy and comfortable, and allows you to breathe. Once you apply a good enough standard to some of the expectations that tie you in knots, you'll free yourself to enjoy your life more.

Adventures In Gymnastics

About five years ago, I suddenly realized—or *finally* realized, depending on who you talk to, me or my husband—that running my own business was a huge endeavor.

When I began to travel more, and had less time at home, it was hard to justify spending it in the kitchen, especially since my interest in cooking was limited to begin with.

I looked for alternatives to spending precious hours preparing meals. My first idea was a bartering arrangement with a friend. She and I cooked meals for each other's families two nights a week, so that we both had to cook less.

The first week I sent over nourishing hot meals, prepared with love. But, by the fourth week, it was canned soup and peanut butter sandwiches, prepared in a hurry. Shortly after that we agreed to stop cooking for each other. That decision probably saved our friendship.

After several other unsuccessful attempts at solving the cooking problem, we were back where we started. I still had a growing business that needed my attention, and a family that still wanted to eat.

Then, one day, the tension between my husband and I that had been simmering, boiled over. I remember exactly how it happened. I'd gone to Boston to give a speech. I had just returned to my hotel room when the phone rang. "Oh, how sweet," I thought. "Alan wants to hear how my program went."

Instead, I heard a loud, angry voice on the other end. "Where's dinner?!" he yelled into to the phone.

Caught off guard, but never at a loss for words, I yelled back, "Just a minute! I'll FAX it to you!!"

It was clear we had to talk. So, when I got home, that's what we did.

→

Finally after years of bickering, we were ready to settle the "Who's doing the cooking?" issue.

The conversation got off to a rocky start. I reminded him how his three sisters had always helped his mother, who, by the way, also had a housekeeper four days a week, which might account for how she was able to get dinner on the table every night. (He really hates it when I bring this up, so I save it for special occasions.)

He countered by reminding me that "normal couples" enjoy cooking together, and that I withheld crucial information when I didn't tell him about my "cooking neurosis" on our first date.

Once we stopped hurling accusations at each other, which wasn't easy, we came up with what we thought was a brilliant and slightly radical solution. We would ask my mother cook for us. She lived only twenty minutes away, loved to cook, and was always sending food home with us anyway.

"Mom," we said, "how would you feel about becoming a private caterer for us—cooking some entrees, putting them in meal-size containers, and letting us fill the trunk of our car with them?" She said "Yes!" (Sorry. She doesn't want me to give out her phone number.)

This turned out to be a very positive arrangement. My mom asks us what we want her to cook, and we end up with ready-to-heat, home-cooked dinners in our freezer. Now when I travel, I feel better knowing that my husband and daughter are eating well.

But, I confess, some days, I feel guilty about not having a legacy of nourishing food to pass on to my daughter. *Maybe I've given up on being the perfect cook. But, I've still got room to obsess about being the perfect mother.* →

So I've devised another radical solution, again with my husband's help. Whenever we go to a dinner party, Alan takes his camera. I ask the hostess if I can help by serving a platter of food. And while I'm holding the platter, my husband snaps a picture.

Then, back at home, I put the photo in a scrapbook I'm making for my daughter. Years from now—when she's in therapy—she'll show her therapist this scrapbook and say, "She *must* have cooked! I've got *hundreds* of pictures like these! I just can't remember what any of her food *tastes* like!"

Some women make dinner. I make scrapbooks.

Update: Two months ago my husband gave me a most unexpected gift. He offered to do the cooking with our daughter, if I agreed to do the shopping and help with the cleanup!

So far, his dinners have been, well, *interesting*. But, I'm going to praise his efforts and keep quiet about the cuisine, because I'm so grateful that he's doing the cooking. And so far, there have been several benefits. My husband seems happier, I've lost 5 pounds eating mostly salad every night, and my daughter is learning that domestic roles aren't carved in stone. ▲

We all know that the superwoman myth is dead. But, long after debunking the myth, we still measure ourselves against an unrealistic yardstick. We compare ourselves to media images, to other women, to our own mothers, all the while trying to reassure ourselves that we are doing a good job.

◄••►

What really makes us crazy is that we constantly try to do the right thing, even when the definition of "right" keeps changing! We need to turn our attention from doing the right thing to spending more time defining what's "good enough." Let's aim for realistic, rather than idealized standards, so that we can do our best—not compulsively, but compassionately—with a minimum of guilt.

It comes down to this: superwoman may not live at your house anymore. But, until you file a card at the post office that says, "No longer at this address," you'll keep getting her mail.

STRENGTH: *Firm Up Those Muscles!*

Meet two attractive women who exude warmth and positive energy. Both are married with children. Both hold jobs that involve dealing with lots of people. And both are "allergic" to conflict of any kind.

When the first woman encountered some "unpleasantness" with another mother in her child's class, she initially acted as though nothing was wrong. Then, without explanation, she started to avoid the woman, strategically enlisting her husband to handle all necessary contacts. He became the "front man" for all car pool arrangements, play dates, and outings. Amazingly, she managed to dodge her "feared foe" for nearly a year. This took some planning! It probably helped that she had twelve years managerial experience to draw from.

The second woman was an employee of mine. Two weeks after I hired her, she announced that she was "conflict averse." (A little bit of therapy can be a dangerous thing.) She expected us to work side by side, day after day, without disagreement or tension. What a handy way to control another person's behavior! She lasted three months.

Many of us have weak muscles when it comes to resolving conflicts with others. Because exercising those muscles causes discomfort, we avoid using them.

Plus, there's confusion about what these muscles are supposed to do.

◄••►

A woman who got divorced after 18 years of marriage told me she should have been more aggressive in her marriage. "Don't you mean more assertive?" I asked. "No," she replied. "My husband wouldn't have heard *assertive*."

I seriously doubt she could have saved her marriage by violating her husband's rights while asserting hers, which is what aggression is. My guess is she had waited too long to stand up for her rights. And now she wanted to hit her ex-husband over the head with them.

Assertiveness is faster, more efficient, and much clearer. You speak up for yourself and set limits on what to do for others. Once you let people know what you want and need, you'll feel happier and better able to meet the demands of daily life. And once you start turning down the most impossible demands on your time, you'll have more energy for the people and priorities that matter.

Assertive means that you:

1. Know what you feel and what you want.
2. Take definite and clear action to present your views.
3. Make sure you are heard fully.
4. Respect the rights of others.

Why do we balk at being assertive? Many women fear that if they do speak up or take action, the situation will only get worse. For example, if you think your husband will get mad if you ask him to help more at home, you may rationalize, "I'll have to clean up anyway, plus I'll have the additional stress of calming him down or putting up with an angry person."

And let's face it, these fears are not totally unwarranted. Strong women like actress Sharon Stone and Attorney General Janet Reno, are seen by some as overly aggressive, because they come across as forceful, no-nonsense women. Society doesn't quite yet know what to do with women like them, other than assign them names like "dragon lady" or worse.

I got some advice from a video producer a couple of years ago. He said, "Paula, when you walk into the room where you're going to speak, and you want the audio visual team (which is usually all male) to make some important technical changes, remember this: to get what you want, you must walk a fine line between being firm and friendly, and a bitch."

I cringed at his comment, partly because I thought he was criticizing me, and partly because his view is shared by so many men. You see, a man can get away with issuing orders. He can *skip* the friendly part. But, a woman must soften her approach, or she'll be judged as "difficult" or "menopausal."

Now, whenever I work with a new AV person, I get acquainted by telling him the "story of the video producer who gave me some great advice a couple of years ago . . . " I put dramatic emphasis on the last word, "bitch." Then, I smile sweetly and add, "So far, I've had good results with just being firm and friendly." Works like a charm!

What are the consequences of not speaking up for yourself? First, your stress level rises. Soon, you are constantly reacting to whatever is thrown at you, which depletes your energy. You get worn down under the demands from family, friends, and colleagues. Your resentment grows, and even the smallest request from a husband or child begins to feel like an enormous burden.

Now you're quick to anger and may snap at the kids and your husband, or just tune them out. You can't give the children the time and attention they need, and you're more critical. Not surprisingly, you may develop health problems, such as headaches and ulcers.

Tough choice, huh? Either speak up, or spiral downward into *stress hell!*

Let's see if you're a member of what I call the "Wipe Your Feet On Me Club." The club's membership numbers in the thousands. Its goal? To go out of existence. But, as long as there are women who join—even though it costs them dearly—the club will stay open.

To maintain an active membership, you must:

Say "yes" too much and then resent others for asking.
You believe that if they hadn't asked, you wouldn't be feeling so miserable now. People have learned that when you're dragging around on the verge of exhaustion, that's their cue to ask for more. Because time and again you've showed them you won't say "no!"

Simmer and stew rather than deal with your anger directly and soon enough.
"Let 'em guess what's wrong," is your motto. And until they do, you'll make them suffer. You've got endless ways to do this: biting sarcasm, accusatory looks and remarks, pouting, saying "Nothing's wrong" when asked (even though you're standing on a chair with a noose

around your neck), withholding sex, "forgetting" to make dinner or "accidentally" burning it. . . .

Take care of others and neglect your needs.
Nurses, mental health practitioners, teachers, and martyrs are particularly adept at this. They believe that they are the caretakers of the *world*, not just their little piece of it. Giving "selflessly" to others has become a habit they desperately need to control. They often suffer from physical ailments and poor health, which means that others end up taking care of *them*.

Are you still paying dues? Or have you happily let your membership lapse? It's up to you.

THE TOUGHEST WORD FOR WOMEN

Why is "no" so hard to say?

- "He won't like me."
- "I'll feel guilty."
- "They'll get angry."
- "I'll hurt her feelings."

Sounds familiar? Many of us worry that we're not "being nice" if we set limits with people. It's no wonder. Most of us are graduates of the school run by Our Sisters of Perpetual Pleasers.

If you've read the books about assertiveness, attended training classes on how to be more assertive, and you're still afraid to speak up, maybe this will motivate you: our daughters tend to follow our lead and inherit not only the inability to say "no," but the low self-esteem that is at its core. And, as you know, kids with low self-esteem are at risk for all kinds of problems as teenagers. We are healthier role models, especially for young girls, if we demonstrate our limits on a daily basis in a firm way.

Having the strength and skill to set limits with our bosses, partners, children, mothers—and often, with ourselves—is essential for any woman who lives and works on the balance beam.

Can you remember the last time you said "no"? When was it? Today? Yesterday? Can't remember?

Who did you say "no" to? And did you say it clearly? Or, did you end up retracting it, or apologizing for it?

If you want to hear someone say "no" and mean it, listen to a two-year-old. Within three minutes (or less) you will hear an unequivocal, no-holds-barred, "NO!"

Adults are more squeamish. We've developed a huge repertoire of ways to *not quite* say it. The following lines are classics.

"I'm very sorry, but I've got a previous engagement."
Translation: Liar, liar, pants on fire!

"I promised my husband I wouldn't take on any more commitments right now."
Translation: Pass the buck and duck for cover.

"Sure, sounds great! I'll call you!" You never hear from her or she says *"yes"* and then cancels at the last minute.
Translation: Hasn't said an honest "no" since she was two years old (see previous page).

"Before I say yes, let me check on one thing . . ."
Translation: She's hoping for a better offer.

"No, I don't mind, really."
Translation: She's just a girl who can't say "no."

"I'll take care of it."
Translation: She lulls the "enemy" into a false sense of security; has no intention of ever "taking care of it."

What makes it confusing for honest people like us is that a response like "I'm very sorry, but I've got a previous engagement" could also be *true*! I tend to believe and respect women who are clear and firm, and avoid false enthusiasms like "I love karaoke parties, but . . ."

Read the following limit-setting statements aloud. How does it feel to say and hear them?

"I'm tempted to say yes—it sounds like fun—but I'm going to have to pass this time."

"I can't. We always spend Friday evening as a family."

"I'm so honored that you asked me. But, this is an especially busy week. Unfortunately, I won't be able to fit it in."

◀•••▶

In the first one, you get the message that your friend wants to spend time with you. But notice, she didn't offer elaborate explanations or excuses.

The second comes from a woman I know, who sets aside one night a week for her family, no matter what. She makes no apologies for sticking to her priorities. And, she's not concerned about being nice.

And the third example demonstrates a gracious way to turn down a request to volunteer your time. This woman's style is to soften her refusal with "I'm so honored that you asked me." It's not required, but it usually helps to maintain good will and is a time-honored tradition in our society.

I've discovered another way to say no, that I use with my own family. Maybe this idea will help you with yours.

Have you ever noticed that you can't get through a day without someone asking you, "Do you know where such and such is?" Doesn't it drive you nuts that people are always asking you to find their stuff?!

I'm going to let you in on a little known fact. There's an anatomical reason why everyone counts on us to find things. *Our uteruses are tracking devices.*

That's right. Just by thrusting out our lower abdomens and scanning the room, we can locate misplaced glasses, lunch boxes, children, all sorts of valuables!

Why not use this information to your advantage? Turn your special gift into a small business. The next time someone asks you where something is, hand them this card:

PERSONAL TRACKING SERVICES
"We Aim To Find What You're Looking For"
DOMESTIC RATE CARD *

Children's belongings: Free for children 5 and under. Starting at age 6, each item costs 25 cents. An annual increase of 25 cents per item will be applied through age 12.

Teenagers' belongings: $3.00 per item. If tracker has to search in teen's room, add 200% to the fee.

Husband's belongings: $10.00 per item: shirts and pants billed at a flat monthly rate of $50.00 to cover daily questions like, "Honey, have you seen my . . ?"

Husband's mail: charge based on date received: $1.00 per envelope for mail received within past week; $5.00 per envelope for mail received in the past month; $25 minimum for mail received within the past decade.

Household items: $5.00 per item: includes large appliances like the dishwasher and washing machine, which are particularly hard items for some people to find.

Items stored in garage or attic: $10.00 per item if stored in labeled boxes. Loose items billed at hourly rate of $75.00. Anything stored beyond five years will be billed at the "Archive" rate of $100 per item. (It may take us days to find it.)

Note: An additional 25% fee will be added to all rush orders such as car keys, lunches, school books, and briefcases.

*Ask us about our introductory offer for executives and managers! We specialize in tracking down misfiled items.

◄••►

You can learn to say "no," and you can say it with style. Stop thinking that saying "no" means that you're weak—"I'm lazy, disorganized, and selfish!"—and realize how much strength you gain when you say it.

LEARNING TO SAY "NO"

For many people, saying no is the first step toward a positive vision of themselves: This is what I want; this is who I am. When you're able to say "no" effectively and clearly, you're affirming the values you hold most dear.

First, let go of thinking you *should* say "yes" and start thinking that you will *choose* to say "yes" or *choose* to say "no." Declaring your real wants and desires as *choices* makes them a lot clearer.

Second, assess how important the "No" is to you. According to Bobbie Reed, author of *Pleasing You is Destroying Me*, the Big Nos (such as turning down a major expectation of your husband, boss, child or best friend) are the toughest, because they have the greatest consequences for the relationships. Medium Nos are the decisions we deal with daily (requests from family, friends, and coworkers). Little Nos (invitations from acquaintances, solicitations from strangers, and good causes of all kinds) needn't cause us anxiety, but often do.

It's a tremendous relief to master the art of saying "no" to phone solicitors. And, it's incredibly simple. All you do is say, "I don't accept phone solicitations," and hang up.

Or, you can have fun with them. Here are some ideas sent to me by my friend, Judith:

1. If they say they're John Doe from the XYZ Company, ask them to spell their name. Then, ask them to spell the company name. Next, ask them where it's located. Continue asking nit-picking questions for as long as it takes for them to hang up.

2. Crying out, in a well-simulated tones of pleasure and surprise, "Sharon!! Is this really you? Oh, my god! Sharon, how have you BEEN?" Hopefully this will give Sharon a few brief moments of terror as she try figures out how the hell she could have known you.

3. If that phone service calls trying to get you to sign up with their Friends and Family plan, reply, in as sinister a voice as you can muster, "I don't have any friends. Would you be my friend?"

4. Tell the telemarketer you are busy and if he will give you his phone number, you will call him back. If he says he isn't allowed to give out his number, ask for his home number and tell him you will call him at home . . . at dinner time. (This is usually the most effective method for getting rid of telemarketers.)

If saying "no" is uncomfortable for you, write down the following statements on a card. Then, if you're in a jam and don't know what to say, you've got a handy pocket reference: remember, done right, saying "no" shows consideration for others—and for yourself.

- "That's an excellent offer, but I'm afraid I'll have to pass on it for the time being."
- "I'd love to say "yes," but I can't right off the bat. Give me some time to see if I can work something out."
- "It just won't work for us."
- "That's not something I do." (This phrase is often used by celebrities who don't want to give autographs. I met a singer who said this and then added, "But may I give you a hug?")
- Delivered sympathetically but firmly, "Gee, I'm sorry you have that problem," and then keeping quiet, brings a manipulative, guilt-producing person to a complete stop.
- "No." At times the best way to say no is to simply say it.

WISE WOMEN AT WORK

Saying "no" to your boss is a dreaded communication for many women. How do you say it? Some people do it by procrastinating.

Maybe the task is unpleasant or too large or complicated. So, you keep putting it off, secretly hoping the boss will change his mind, and you won't have to do it. Hey! Maybe he'll ask someone else to do it!

The best way to say "no" to your boss is to *negotiate*.

When you're stressed to the point where you're starting to hate your job, and you can't afford to quit, what should you do?

You should start by cutting yourself some emotional slack. Dana Friedman, co-president of the Families and Work Institute in New York

City, says in *Working Mother* magazine, "You've watched friends and colleagues lose their jobs and you're probably worried about your own security."

Second, recognize your value to the company. Don't be afraid to discuss your work load with your boss. Just do it in a constructive way.

Show her how the company would benefit by rethinking your duties. Document how your work load has increased. (What additional duties did you take on? How much time do they take?)

Concentrate on the inefficiencies that are created by your ever-increasing work load. (Do you have enough time for essential planning? Do customers feel short-changed because you have to rush through your tasks?)

Consult with a friendly co-worker and brainstorm ways to streamline the department's work load. (Are there duties that could be eliminated or reassigned? Could the work be reorganized? Does the flow of work make sense?)

Then try to translate your findings to bottom line results. Would everyone be more productive if certain tasks were eliminated? Could the company save money by hiring a temp to do some of the routine tasks?

Once you've done your homework, meet with your boss. Let her know you understand the current business environment is tough and find out whether she sees any relief in sight. If not, propose some of your solutions as a way of preserving the company's profitability in rugged economic times.

It is possible to say what you want without blaming, feeling put down, or feeling guilty. You can say "no" and still be a team player.

Adventures In Gymnastics

An executive assistant was so overwhelmed by the work on her desk that by 2:00 PM, she would, in her words, go "brain dead." Routinely working12-hour days, she would come home to her live-in companion and disappear into a sullen huff. During the night, she'd awaken to worry about unfinished tasks.

Frantic, she and a fellow assistant asked their boss if they could bring in a professional organizer. Several months later she still works too many hours, but she's organized the way she handles tasks, arranged for more predictable hours and carved out time for a home life.

She says, "If you aren't at home and can't devote time to your relationship, that starts deteriorating too, and you have nowhere you can have peace. Now that I feel more in control in the office, I can have fun at home." ▲

What if you wanted to avail yourself of the flexible work arrangements your company offers? But, you've got one of those managers who is ambivalent about flextimers.

What would a wise woman do? That's right—she'd negotiate.

Here's some good advice from the "Managing Your Career" column in the *Wall Street Journal*.

Don't just ask for favors. Put together a proposal—complete with performance goals—that meets both your needs and the company's.

Make your manager your best friend. Converse frequently in person or by phone, fax or e-mail about what you're doing and the progress you're making. This will make him or her more comfortable with a lower level of monitoring and control.

Stay abreast of developments. It's easy for flextimers to get left behind as priorities and projects shift.

Be creative. Just because you're tele-commuting or working part-time doesn't mean you can't identify and solve key problems or volunteer for the important projects.

Adjust your schedule in an emergency. Make sure that home and family commitments aren't so great that you can't lend an extra hand when it's needed.

IT'S JUST A MATTER OF TIME

Your time is your most valuable commodity. Let it slip through your fingers, let others steal it from you, and you will become an easy mark for the "Time Thieves."

Got a boss that makes a habit of wasting your time? When she comes in to chat, say right up front, "I'm working on the XYZ project and will have something on your desk by 5:00 PM, if I'm not interrupted." Message: "If you take up my time, you may not get my report." Be sure to keep your tone of voice firm and respectful.

During the peak of my writing schedule for this book, I needed to protect myself from wasting precious time on the phone. So, I e-mailed friends with this message: "Hi! Would love to talk. Let's do it by e-mail for the next 3 weeks, so I can save my 'juice' for writing." As a result of sending that message, I received lots of supportive greetings, funny cartoons and good gossip. And I read them at odd hours when I needed a social boost.

"Can you spare a minute?" Don't get sucked in. This type won't stop when the clock has run for 60 seconds. Say, "Sure, I can spare a minute. When time runs out, look at your watch again and say, "Gee, I really can't spend more than a minute on this right now. Can we schedule another time to talk?" Then pull out your calendar and book her for another time.

Study your own habits. Do you regularly visit other people's offices and waste their time? Perhaps because you visit them, they feel they should also be visiting you. If you cut down your drop-in visits, they will too. Save friendly chats for lunch time.

When people call, set the tone for the conversation. Steer clear of phrases like "What's up?" if you don't have time to find out. Open-ended questions like that will get you long-winded answers. Instead, keep your voice friendly and say, "What can I do for you?" or "How can I help you?"

Those questions prompt your caller to get straight to the point.

The best time saver I've learned recently is to call people back after work hours. Since many of my clients always have their voice mail on and are rarely at their desks, why use valuable daytime hours to leave messages? So, now I make a round of phone calls between five and six at night. And the next morning, they call me back!

What can happen if you set "firm, but flexible" policies about your time and stick to them? Debra Thompson, an Arizona consultant-trainer and mother of five can tell you. She refuses Saturday night stays if they interfere too much with family life. She once lost a client over the issue.

However, she tries to combine several trips into one and offers discounts to clients who are willing to book appointments to coincide with others nearby. By doing so, her flexibility benefits her clients' checkbooks, and her firmness benefits her family.

HOME IS WHERE THE OFFICE IS

The saying goes, "Home is where the heart is." Today, many of us would have to admit that home is where the *office* is. We may *think* we're home, but our thoughts wander to the business day behind us, instead of focusing on the family in before us. Our bedrooms look like office supply stores, with phones, fax machines, and computers at our fingertips.

Like lava flowing down a mountain endangering a village, work oozes out of the office, threatening to wipe out your personal time. You must either stop it or get out of its way. That involves not only setting limits with other people; it involves setting limits in your *own mind*.

Can you leave work at work? Or does it come home with you every night, encroaching upon your thoughts or plans?

It doesn't matter whether you commute on the freeway or climb fourteen steps from your basement. To enjoy a full life, you've got to make a successful transition from work to home each day.

If your office is in your home, you've got special challenges, because your work may always be a few feet away. Having an office within your periphery doesn't work for most women. It certainly didn't work for me. Until we moved my office out of the main living quarters and onto a separate floor, I couldn't set firm boundaries between my work day and my family life.

After physical boundaries, mental boundaries are the most important . . . and the most challenging. Women who work at home must protect their boundaries from the moment they sit down at their desks.

Remember Cathy from the cartoon by Cathy Guisewite? Here's a typical morning in her home office:

"Hi, Cathy. What are you doing?"
"It's 9:00 AM. I'm working."
" . . . Hi Cathy. What are you doing?"
"It's 9:15 AM. I'm trying to work."
" . . . Hi Cathy. What are you doing?"
"It's 9:30 AM. I'm attempting to work!"

◄••►

"Hi, Cathy. What are you doing?"

" . . . It's 9:45 AM! I'm ripping the phone out of the wall! Nobody thinks I'm really working, so people like you interrupt me all day long!"

"The woman in the TV commercial isn't so cranky."

"The woman in the TV commercial only has to sustain it for 30 seconds."

You may have some fantasies about what it's like to work at home. So, let's take a closer look at what it's really like.

Yes, you can wear what you want. (I've conducted radio interviews and booked speaking engagements in my bathrobe.) Theoretically, you can work when you want, stop when you want, and even take a nap if you want.

You can stop work to get your kids off to school and have breakfast with your husband. And after school, your kids can do their homework in your office, so that you can spend extra time together.

But, that's where paradise ends, and the real work starts.

You can also spend an hour on the phone just getting supplies, copies, and postage to mail one package. There are days when your fax machine is jammed, your printer's frozen, your modem needs an upgrade, and tech support is $100 an hour.

Friends and family are asked to call only at certain times. They "forget" and call when it's convenient for *them*.

Once you've dealt with all of these intrusions and diversions, you must call it a day, no matter how much or how little you've accomplished. *That's* the hard part.

Wherever I speak, I collect ideas on how to leave the work day behind. Here are some inspirational ideas from some inspired women:

- One in Corpus Christi *takes off her bra*.
- Another from Fort Worth *gardens*.
- *Exercising* works for a woman in Seattle.
- Many women *sing in their cars*—LOUDLY.
- A Cleveland woman *tucks the comics* in her briefcase and reads them on the bus.
- *Playing with her pet* is the way a Minneapolis woman winds down.
- *Something sweet* wraps it up for a Kalamazoo woman.
- Another in Chicago *writes down her work problems* on a piece of paper, and puts the paper in an envelope marked "Do Not Open Until Tomorrow Morning." Then she seals the envelope, tucks it in her drawer and leaves, feeling unburdened and ready to enjoy her evening.
- A CEO from Los Angeles *"parks" her work troubles* by a roadside stand she passes on the way home. She leaves them there overnight and then picks them up on her way into to work the next morning.
- And my personal favorite: a consultant from New Orleans *locks her desk at the end of each business day*. Then, she slowly backs out of her office pointing to the desk and repeating, 'STAY!" (It's working. So far, the desk hasn't followed her home.)

◄••►

Think of at least *two ways* you can let go of the "remains" of the day. Jot them down and stick them on your office wall or on your dashboard as a reminder to use them.

Strength: *Nobody Does It Better...*

A good friend of mine recently celebrated her 50th birthday. To mark this milestone, she gave herself a magnificent gift—a trip to Paris. I went over to her house to wish her bon voyage.

"I've got to go!" Sarah exclaimed the moment I arrived. "I have a two-hour packing marathon ahead of me, and then I've got to go back to my office!"

"I thought you were packed," I said.

"I am. Now I need for pack for Allison."

"Why are your packing for Allison?" I asked. "She doesn't leave for a week!" (My friend had given herself the added treat of a week in France on her own, before her husband and daughter joined her.)

"I'd rather do it myself," she replied.

"But, Sarah, you're rushing around like a maniac! You haven't slept for days, your back's acting up, and the doctor just prescribed an anti-anxiety medicine for you. These are *not* signals that you should pack for your eleven-year-old!"

"I know," she said, avoiding eye contact with me.

Trying to help, I said, "Why don't you leave a list for Mark? He and Allison can pack together."

◀•••▶

"Want to know the truth?" she asked.

"Yes," I said. "And so would my readers." (I'd given her fair warning that anything she said might end up in my book. I also promised to change the names in this story to protect the innocent.)

"I don't trust Mark to follow my instructions. He'll forget or bring the wrong clothes."

"So what's the big deal if Allison *doesn't* bring the right clothes? I understand they sell them in Paris."

"But, this is for a *month*. And they need to be drip-dry. It's all very complicated . . ."

"You're right, I'd forgotten." I said, hugging her good-bye. "Nobody packs better than you. In fact, the next time I take a trip, I'm going to have *you* pack for *me*! Thank goodness you're stepping in, before Allison learns how to pack. It could have been disastrous!!"

She laughed and went into the house, no doubt to pack her daughter's suitcase.

Want to know how to grow dependent people? Just do what my friend did: rush in and rescue capable people from learning how to become resourceful and competent. Results are guaranteed.

Here's a well-known folk song about a married couple, Henry and Liza, who have a problem: there's a hole in a bucket.

◀• ▶

There's a hole in the bucket, dear Liza, dear Liza. There's a hole in the bucket, dear Liza, a hole.
Then fix it, dear Henry, dear Henry, dear Henry. Then fix it, dear Henry, dear Henry, fix it.

With what shall I fix it, dear Liza, dear Liza? With what shall I fix it, dear Liza, with what?
With straw, dear Henry, dear Henry. With straw, dear Henry, dear Henry, with straw.

The whole refrain is repeated through each question and answer . . .

The straw is too long . . . Then cut it . . .
With what shall I cut it . . . With a knife . . .
The knife is too dull . . . Then sharpen it . . .
*On what shall I sharpen it . . . On a **stone** . . .*
*The stone is too dry . . . Then **wet it** . . .*
*With what shall I wet it . . . With **water** . . .*
*In what shall I fetch it . . . **IN A BUCKET !!!** . . .*

and ends up with . . .

There's a hole in the bucket, dear Liza, dear Liza. There's a hole in the bucket, dear Liza, a hole.
Then fix it, dear Henry, dear Henry, dear Henry . . .
(author unknown)

Did you notice how the more Henry asked for help, the shorter Liza's temper got? What would have happened if Liza had stopped after the *first*

◄••►

question and said, *"I'm sorry to hear about your bucket, Henry. How do you propose to fix it?"*

Sure, Henry might need to brainstorm with Liza for a few minutes, but then she could say, "Well, you've come up with several possible solutions. Give them a try and let me know how they're working."

Calm and matter-of-fact. Available, but not over-involved. Encouraging instead of discouraging. That's Liza, the delegator.

Just replace the name Henry with your children's, partners', co-workers', and even friends', and you'll see why we feel overwhelmed. We cultivate dependent people and then resent it when they come to us for help!

CONTROL AND THE ILLUSION OF POWER

To let go of the responsibility, you also have to let go of the control. Judith Viorst describes Dana, a manager, in her book *Imperfect Control: Our Lifelong Struggles with Power and Surrender*. Dana is driving herself and all her employees nuts, because she simply cannot delegate power.

> *"Dana is down in the mailroom making certain that the mail is properly sorted. She is also in the washroom making certain that Central Supply has bought the right soap. She is also going from desk to desk, monitoring everybody's phone calls, shaking her head or writing a say-this note, or maybe suicidally drawing a finger across her throat if she decides that the phone call is going badly."*

Viorst observes that Dana doesn't really need a competent staff. All she really needs are a dozen cloned Danas. "Only with clones could Dana overcome her reluctance to delegate authority. Dana is one version of that familiar workplace nemesis—the control freak," says the author.

There are overconfident, I-know-best control freaks. And there are tormented, anxious, one-false-move-and-I'm-dead control freaks. Viorst says some people control because they are afraid of failure. Others control "because of a sense of inadequacy, hoping to build themselves up (or at least to protect themselves from ridicule or rejection) by taking over." And then there are the control freaks who enjoy the "heady rush of power" that simply feeling in control provides.

Most likely, you know if you're a control freak. And you will *definitely* know when you're around one. Just look over your shoulder and there they'll be, telling you how to do things, even after they have "delegated" the job to you.

I ask my audiences this question, "How many of you want to work with people who can't think on their own, act on their own, or come up with solutions on their own?" No hands go up.

"Now, how many of you want to work with resourceful problem solvers, who can take certain tasks off your hands, so that you can focus on what's important?" Every hand shoots up.

Then I say, "The only way you're going to groom people for that is by learning to DELEGATE! How many of you are willing to do that?"

Now, only about half the hands go up, and people raise them slowly and tentatively. *Why is that?*

Because people know that delegation is a skill that requires practice. And because they know what's involved, it may seem easier to do the job themselves.

Typically, you may catch yourself making the following excuses to hold onto tasks:

- I don't have time to train.
- No one else will do it correctly.
- I like this job. So, I'll do it.
- This is an awful job. I can't give it to anyone else.

Plus, you may find that you have some concerns about losing authority and possibly, your identity.

Adventures In Gymnastics

About a year ago, I returned home exhausted, after several days away on a business trip. When I opened the door, I began to weep. Newspapers were strewn everywhere. Plates and cups covered the coffee tables. Mail was piled high, and there was nowhere to sit down. I wanted to turn around and get right back on that airplane. →

Instead, I realized that the time had come to delegate some of the things I normally do when I'm home with my family. This idea was met with about as much enthusiasm as a trip to the dentist.

But, little by little, my husband and daughter learned to keep the household running while I was away. It took time, patience, and training over several months.

Then, one evening I returned home from another business trip. I opened the door. Once again, I began to weep. But this time it was for different reasons. The living room was clean and inviting. A fire was blazing in the fireplace. From the kitchen came the wonderful aroma of fresh baked banana bread . . . WAIT A MINUTE! HOLD THE PHONE! I never taught them how to make *banana bread!*

Suddenly, I felt very unsure of who I was or what my role was. If they could do everything I could do *and* make banana bread, *maybe they didn't need me anymore!*

It was a painful feeling. I got over it.

You may feel vulnerable when letting go of something that has always been in your domain. It's become part of your identity. But delegation, done well, shouldn't take away from your strengths and abilities. It will simply free up needed time for your other pursuits or responsibilities. Instead of clinging to a task you already know how to do, use the time you gain to learn something new. ▲

Delegation: the person who is responsible for delivering results, decides how the job gets done. As the delegator, you'll have input in the

◄••►

beginning, when you discuss the expected results and the timeline. But, whether it's at home or at the office, once you delegate, your role is to offer support and encourage independent, resourceful action. If you focus on HOW the person will accomplish the task, you're sabotaging delegation.

Delegation begins by matching the person's skills to the right task. For instance, you wouldn't ask a six-year-old to wash your car if you wanted a detailed job. Nor would you ask a temporary employee to run an important meeting. Success is often determined at the start, when you match up the right person with the right job.

A good rule of thumb is that the person with the most skill takes the lead on a particular task. However, if that person doesn't want to take it on, there are alternatives to delegation. You could:

1. Hire an outside source or person to do the job.
2. Negotiate to change the job.
3. Barter with someone to do the job.
4. Eliminate the job altogether.

Which alternative is best depends on the people involved and the situation. For example, one woman bartered with her retired neighbors to mow their lawn when they were gone in the summer in exchange for ten days of emergency child care during the school year.

When I was first married, I paid the family bills. Then, as I got busier, my husband and I re-negotiated, and he took over. Two years later, he negotiated for a bookkeeper, because my business finances—in addition to the

◄••►

family's—were too much for him to manage. It's common for the best person to do the job to change, as the scope of the job changes.

Remember the Roll Juggling Exercise earlier? Take a look at the roles you placed in the bag marked "Roles to delegate, negotiate, or eliminate." Think about what you want to do with each of these roles. Then, write down your plan of action below:

One role I will delegate is _____.

One role I will negotiate is _____.

One role I will eliminate is _____.

One role I will barter is_____.

Other roles I want to reconsider: _____.

So, there you have it: **delegate or get deluged.** Yes, it's hard to delegate work, when there's no one left in your department. And, it's maddening at home, when your kids pretend they're all thumbs, or didn't hear you, or didn't understand what you asked, or didn't realize that you wanted it done *this* year. But, your kids won't be leaving until they're 18. So, learn to delegate, do it often, and follow these guidelines:

- Keep your expectations clear.
- Clarify the aims and deadlines of the project
- Set up a procedure for reporting progress.
- Ask to hear any concerns or questions before the person starts.

STRENGTH: *Even Pros Use a Spotter*

Before we go any further, stand up, click your heels together and repeat, "There's no harm in asking. There's no harm in asking. There's no harm in asking . . ."

Eleven percent of women in high-powered positions—a group that tends to keep their stress to themselves—ask for help when they need it, one study reported. Another that included full-time mothers and those who work outside of the home, cited 23 percent. Neither number is very impressive, considering how few women this is. Apparently, we think there *is* harm in asking!

What's the big deal with asking for help? Is it a big deal for *you*?

Take a moment to think about the last time you asked for help. Who did you ask? What did you ask for? What did they say?

Couldn't come up with a recent example? There's a good chance you're uncomfortable with asking for help. And, if you're OK with asking for help, but people often turn you down, you need to change your approach.

Remember part two of the phrase, "There's no harm in asking?" It goes like this: "All they can do is say no." Worrying that your request will be turned down is the number one reason women don't ask for help. You rationalize, "He'll just say no, anyway."

Why the mental maneuvering? To avoid *conflict*. If you dread the possibility of conflict even *more* than you dread being turned down, you probably won't ask for help.

Other thoughts and feelings that get in the way of asking for help or asking for it effectively:

- *If feeling dependent scares you* . . . you manipulate other people, rather than being direct, so that you don't feel like you're really *asking* for help.
- *If you believe that needing help is a sign of weakness* . . . you deny that you need help and become angry and resentful; this is how martyrs are made.
- *If you think, "I shouldn't have asked."* . . . you feel unworthy of others' support or are afraid of being a burden; low self-esteem is at its roots.
- *If you're afraid that the person you ask will be angry/upset/critical* . . . you act timid and meek, either apologizing for asking ("I hate to ask, but . . .") or don't ask for what you want, and end up feeling disappointed.

A woman in one of my audiences told this story. She was preparing to move across the state and needed some help with packing. Not wanting to impose on her friends, she put off asking them for as long as possible. When they said "yes," she felt both "grateful and a little uncomfortable."

The following weekend, as her friends packed her fragile china, she kept quiet and didn't offer suggestions on how to protect the dishes from breaking in transit. "They were so generous with their time, I didn't feel like I could tell them what to do."

A week later, she opened the box at her new apartment. In it, she found hundreds of pieces of china . . . really *tiny* pieces.

If you have trouble asking for help, consider how letting others help you is actually a vote of confidence in their abilities. Imagine how good it feels to be on the receiving end of this message: "I know you can do this and I trust you to be responsible. Contrast that message with, "I never ask you because you can't do anything right and you're irresponsible."

Want to watch someone's face light up? The next time they ask you to help them, say, "Thank you for asking. I appreciate your faith in me to do a good job."

New Woman magazine featured an article about how to enlist co-workers' help on the job in an atmosphere where "survival-of-the-fittest" was undermining teamwork. When they asked me how employees could legitimately and tactfully ask for help, I gave them these strategies:

1. Ask for help at the beginning of an assignment. If you wait until you're swamped, co-workers will resent having to rescue you.

2. If you feel your boss will disapprove of your asking for help, go to her first. Ask her permission to approach a co-worker for assistance. Make a case for how your colleague's expertise will contribute to the project. Avoid

sounding apologetic and your boss is likely to value your initiative—and will probably say yes.

3. Approach your co-worker in the same spirit. You don't want her to feel like she got dumped on. Acknowledge that she wasn't expecting to spend time working on your project and try to accommodate her other responsibilities, so that you don't throw her off track.

   IMPORTANT: Emphasize that you feel very fortunate to have her help. And make sure she knows you're going to share the credit when the project is finished.

ALL YOU HAD TO DO WAS ASK

Remember the landmark study from a few years back that found women do 80% of the housework? According to the latest research cited in the book *She Works/He Works*, the figure for dual-income households is now closer to 55%.

Maybe the numbers have improved. But, the fact is, men still must be asked to help. Seeing things that need to be done around the house does not come easy or naturally to them. And I've got proof.

ADVENTURES IN GYMNASTICS

John Grey, author of *Women Are From Venus, Men Are From Mars*, didn't need to do all that research. The main difference between men and women is that women notice a basket of laundry blocking their path, and men don't.

Recently, I had some back problems and needed my husband to carry the laundry up and down the stairs for me. Being a genuinely helpful guy, he agreed to do this.

The next day I mentioned that there were two baskets of laundry ready to be carried downstairs. Just as he had promised, he took them down to the laundry room. There was only one hitch. He did it three days later. I should have recognized this as an omen. Instead, I washed the clothes and optimistically announced that there were two baskets of clean laundry ready to come up from the laundry room.

The sun rose and the sun set. And that was the first day.

On the second day he flew to a meeting and returned that same evening. A frequent flyer myself, I know household chores are not a top priority when you're home for just a few hours. So, I cut him some slack and didn't insist that he bring the baskets upstairs. After all, one more day without bath towels wouldn't kill me. Whatever I was losing in personal hygiene, I was gaining in household support and cooperation.

By the third day, he had carried one basket upstairs. This was good. (If he had waited one more day, I would have been wearing his underwear.) But, there was still the matter of the second laundry basket, which had found a permanent resting place down in the living room.

Deep in my heart, I knew he would eventually carry that basket of clothes upstairs. But, eventually might be a long, long time. So, I thought I'd prompt him. First, I carefully scooted the laundry to the center of the first step, leaving barely two inches on either side. Then, I stood back to admire my efforts. Satisfied that my barricade would cue him to carry the basket up on his next trip, I went about my morning.

Imagine my surprise when he showed up in the bathroom half an hour later, empty-handed.

"How did you get up here?" I asked.

"What do you mean? I just came up the stairs," he replied.

"Notice anything unusual on the way?"

"Like what?" he asked.

"Like a basket of laundry?" I said.

"Oh, that. I thought I'd better leave it in the living room because I wasn't sure whether the clothes were clean or dirty."

Suddenly, I had a vision. I was throwing books at him, hundreds and hundreds of books about couples' communication. Then, I heard someone shouting. It might have been me.

"But, the laundry basket wasn't *in* the living room! It was in your

→

104

direct path on the stairs! What did you do, *vault* over it?!"

"You're going to put this in your book, aren't you?" he said.

"Yup," I said, as I stepped into the shower. Amazing. Two fresh, clean bath towels appeared within two minutes.

Note: Ever since my husband learned that this story would be included in the book, he's been bringing the laundry down the same day I ask, and carrying it up as soon as it's finished, with only one request from me!

This proves that our partners will tune in and pitch in, *with the right motivation*. Here's how to change your partner's behavior in three easy steps. First, tell him you're going to write a book. (You don't actually have to *write* it; just *talk* about it.) Second, you must write a story about something he does or doesn't do that really bugs you, something he wouldn't want other people to know about. Third, show him the story and say that you're thinking of including it in the book. Now watch closely. Within 24 hours you will witness a miracle! ▲

WHEN NAGGING DOESN'T WORK . . .

Rebecca asked her husband to buy some T-shirts for their twin girls. When she wrote out the directions—where to shop, how many to buy and in what sizes—he protested, "I can't believe you're writing all this out!"

She believes that if she doesn't write everything out, "it's not going to get done." Bewildered that her husband "needs" this kind of direction, she told me, "This is a man who sticks heart catheters into people's coronary

◄••►

arteries and makes life-and-death decisions every day!"

Marcia, a professional and mother of three, divides the household tasks in two, and organizes them for her husband, a psychologist. She doesn't want him to "drop the ball" and says she "knows what he does well and what he doesn't."

It's clear both men have the intelligence to do these tasks. But, can they do them without this kind of supervision?

Rita Derbas, trainer and consultant, who can train *anybody* to do just about *anything*, says "YES!" However, if we're going to get the kind of help we're expecting from the men in our lives, she recommends we change our approach. "Every time we tell our partners not only *what* the task is, but *how* to do it, we undermine our best efforts. What adult *wouldn't* push back at such treatment?"

Instead, she suggests that when you give your partner a job to do, qualify it. "If it needs to be done within a certain time frame, say so. If it involves several steps, mention that, too. But then, back off. Don't tell him *how* to do the task within the allotted time or *how* to organize each step."

The goal is to get our partners to start asking themselves these kinds of questions:

1. What's the most efficient way of doing this?
2. How long is it likely to take?
3. How can I get it done by the time I must be home?
4. Do I have everything I need?

5. What will I do with the kids while I do this?

These are problem-solving skills that our partners *can* learn. But, remember, most men have been reared to think that their main responsibility is breadwinning. How traditional the roles are in the relationship continues to be a major factor in our partners' willingness to do a bigger share of household and child-care duties.

Are you determined to shift the weight of responsibilities at home? Then start by telling your partner this:

"Women's stress from housework tends to be higher than men's because traditionally "female" tasks (meals, laundry) are repetitive and give you little control over when they must be done, unlike typically "male" chores such as yard work and home repairs."(*Parenting*, September 1997.)

One solution would be to equalize things at home by rotating chores so that NEITHER of you is stuck with the high-stress ones all the time. Make a list of everything that needs to be done. Then sit down with your partner and ask, "How can we divide these tasks? I can't do them all myself."

You'll need to be patient, assertive, and respectful, and allow for the time and practice it will take for *both* of you to change your approach to household management. And it's an investment that will yield big rewards.

A final thought . . . about reciprocity: when you ask for help and you get it, you don't necessarily need to return the favor. But, let your partner

◀••▶

know you'll be looking for opportunities to help her or him.

For example, my husband spent 10 years helping me become a business woman, which was a monumental task for both of us. (I had few innate business skills and was more oriented toward *giving* away services than I was to *selling* them.)

In return for his persistence and faith in me, I'm going to spend the next 10 years turning him into a ballroom dancer. If you understood how "unique" his sense of rhythm is, you'd know why I've set aside a decade. Now that I think about it, maybe I should allow eleven years . . . no, twelve . . . no, thirteen . . . .

BALANCE

Staying on the Beam

Balance: *Plant Your Feet Firmly*

It's almost imperceptible. But, look closely. There it is, right after she mounts the balance beam from the springboard and rolls into a somersault. She stands and takes an infinitesimal moment . . . *to get her footing.*

Compared to backhand springs, flips, and leaps, this subtle movement is easy to miss. But, it's vital to her success. That slight shift of her feet prepares her physically and mentally for what comes next.

Do you "plant your feet" before you begin your day? Or do you jump out of bed the minute the alarm rings? Stumbling unsteadily to the kitchen, bleary-eyed and barely awake, you run into the door frame. "Coffee! I need coffee!" you moan. As you start the shower, you gulp down a cup. Three minutes later you're drying off. Suddenly you feel a caffeine-induced power surge. You throw on a robe and go wake the kids. (Whoops! You forgot. You don't *have* any kids. So, you go over to the neighbor's and wake *their* kids.) You're pumped, and you're thinking, "I can do *anything* today!" You'll need a "hit" of caffeine every few hours to sustain your hyper-confidence, so keep your coffee cup handy.

Some people rise, have a leisurely cup of tea, exercise, read the newspaper before facing the day. It's true. I have three friends who pull off this feat off every morning! (It's hard having friends like that.)

More often, I hear stories like the one from Maria Watts in the *San*

◄••►

Francisco Examiner. Before heading to her job as vice president of a small college in the San Francisco Financial District, she meditates while playing Bach or other baroque music. Once behind the wheel, a becalmed Watts tries to conjure up "good thoughts about my fellow drivers."

But, practically every day, just minutes down the road, her serenity is shattered. "Someone speeds or runs a red light or does something threatening, and then you get scared, and your heart beats faster," says Watts. "It takes a while to get back into a peaceful mode, and sometimes, I just can't do it." Frequently, she arrives at work frazzled and on guard.

There are likely to be jolts to our internal environment each day. But, preparing our minds and bodies for unexpected chaos, makes a difference in the long run.

RESOURCES TO COMBAT STRESS

The key to combating stress, according to Kent State University professor, Steven Hobfoll, Ph.D., is developing greater social and personal resources.

Read the statements below. Decide if you agree or disagree with them.

Personal Resources:

- I feel good about myself.
- I feel I have reasonable control over events.
- I am usually optimistic about the future.
- I have adequate physical stamina.

- I have a strong sense of commitment.
- I have adequate finances and tools to meet important goals.

Social Resources:

- I am valued by others.
- I have someone with whom I feel close.
- I have someone on my side to talk to.
- I am comfortable asking for help.
- I have opportunity to gain things I value.
- I provide others with emotional support and help with tasks.

Did you agree with the majority of these statements? Do you have the personal resources that build inner strength and are needed during periods of stress? And what about your social resources, which are necessary for strong, healthy interpersonal relationships? Do you have enough of them?

In a study that asked people to define success, 67% ranked "being in control of your life" as number one, followed by 65%, who said that "having enough time for family and friends" indicated success. Notice how both of these relate to the list above.

Important note: women who are most on top of stress are less likely to overeat, drink alcohol or use other substances to relieve tension. And they are likely to exercise more than people who are stressed out.

Stress is among the top 10 reasons women miss work and one of the primary reasons women seek medical attention.

◀••▶

There's one group that's particularly at risk. The most stressed working women are those who are better educated and have high-status professional positions. They tend to work longer hours and have higher paying and more demanding jobs. Not only do they tend to keep their stress to themselves, they complain of having difficulty getting to sleep, gastrointestinal problems, headaches, and muscle strain.

And, the American Journal of Psychiatry found the suicide rate for professional women—both married and single—was many times greater than the general female population.

The presence or absence of social support, and the quality of the relationships we have, can be significant factors in determining how frequently we become sick and how rapidly we recover.

Studies show that people who receive social support have better blood pressure readings, lower weight, and a 57% lower mortality rate than those who do not receive this kind of support. Simply put, those rich in friends live longer.

FROM THE PEPSI GENERATION TO THE SANDWICH GENERATION

Today 7 million people in the U.S. are acting as unpaid caregivers, 75% of them women. And, there are many more women who don't provide direct care but make arrangements for it. They may not live near their parents, but Mom and Dad are on constantly on their minds.

The Baby Boom generation can expect to be become the most "sandwiched" in history. For the first time, married couples will spend more time

◄••►

caring for a parent than a child.

One woman described herself as "a piece of taffy being pulled on all sides." If you're in this position, expect to feel some anger and guilt; it goes with the territory. Also, get comfortable with asking for help. If other family members aren't doing their share, let them know. Instead of complaining, make specific requests. "I need you to chip in $100" or, "I'll consult the doctor. You make arrangements for the homemaker."

All of us need to develop our personal and social resources and use them wisely. And because life holds both expected and unexpected stress, we must create rituals that allow us to approach each day on *our* terms, not the clock's.

I'm off for a walk now with a friend and afterwards, some time with my family. Writing this section reminded me that I'm in that group of women who experience the greatest amount of stress—a demanding job, a father with Alzheimer's, a mother living alone, and no other family nearby. I'd better stop and take my own advice.

Balance: *Pace Yourself*

Something happened recently, when my husband and daughter were gone for a few days. With only two tasks to focus on, my life took on a simplicity and steady rhythm that I rarely experience. And it was amazing how good it felt.

My main task was to write; I could do it any hour of the night or day. I felt focused, relaxed, and well-rested. (Perhaps I should become one of those reclusive writers, who rents a beach house for months at a time.) It showed that the research is right: **each of us has a definite inner rhythm and a natural pace.** And much of the time, we work *against* it rather than *with* it, causing ourselves more stress, and making tasks more difficult to accomplish.

Think about your ideal day. Let the things that you *have* to do take a back seat to the things you would *choose* to do. Structure your time and activities in a way that would leave you feeling productive but relaxed, and very content with yourself.

On the following page, list the activities for a day. Put down what you would *want the day to be*, not as it normally goes.

Your Ideal Day

TIME	ACTIVITY
7am–8am	
8am–9am	
9am–10am	
10am–11am	
11am–12pm	
12pm–1pm	
1pm–2pm	
2pm–3pm	
3pm–4pm	
4pm–5pm	
5pm–6pm	
6pm–7pm	
7pm–8pm	
8pm–9pm	
9pm–10pm	
10pm–11pm	

What did you notice? Did you:

- focus on many activities or just a few?
- rise earlier or later than you normally do?
- nap?
- exercise?
- prefer to be alone, with others, or a mix of both?

And how did you sustain your energy throughout the day? Was it:

- with coffee or sugar?
- with something that works better for you?

Discovering your natural pace is often a revelation. You learn how much stimulation—compared to how much quiet—you need. You learn how much rest you require. And you learn how much time you like to be alone and how much social interaction you enjoy.

Following our own inner rhythm—rather than marching to a beat that pounds away at us—has several instant benefits. By pacing yourself naturally, you:

1. maintain your energy rather than deplete it.
2. do the right tasks at the right time, based on your energy cycle.
3. pause to replenish yourself without fear of being "lazy."
4. have adequate reserves to deal with unanticipated challenges.

What gets in the way of our balancing our activity level and taking charge of our time?

MULTI-TASKING: TOO MUCH TO BE ASKING?

You know what multi-tasking is. It's when you put on your makeup while driving to work. Or, it's when you talk on the phone while having sex. If you're really advanced, it's when you put on your makeup on your way to work, while having phone sex.

You'll know a multi-tasker when you see one. If you force her to come to a dead stop, you'll notice she can't maintain this single focus without a new thought or movement popping up within a few seconds. Multi-taskers are the ultimate mental jugglers. And some try to juggle as much as they've got on their minds . . . on their plates.

ADVENTURES IN GYMNASTICS

Sandy Flick invented the Lap-Top Commuter after she ruined a new pair of pants while eating a burger and fries on the way home. Inspired by the design of children's car seats, it prevents spills by providing individual compartments for each food and drink item. Wanting to cash in on her idea, she loaded her two children into the car and drove from Middletown, California to Chicago—the first leg of a 10,000 mile marketing trip. She visited the

→

purchasing office of nearly every major fast-food chain and invited the managers out to lunch. According to the *Wall Street Journal,* the lunch consisted of drive-through fare, which she coaxed her guests to eat in the car. As they tested her tray, Ms. Flick drove around, making sharp turns and slamming on the brakes.

What the article doesn't discuss is what happened to those kids in the back seat. Can you imagine? Every time lunch is served, mommy starts driving like a maniac. At the very least it would give you an upset stomach. More than likely, it would make you lose your fries.

I applaud Sandy's spunk and drive, but she had better get to work on a new product for cleaning upchucked lunches. And by the way, feeding your kids burgers and fries, and then making them car sick is a highly effective way to teach them to hate drive-through restaurants.

So, how many things did Sally, the multi-tasking, marketing mom, do at once? If you came up with only three, you're forgetting the fast-food aversion therapy she gave the kids. But, that's OK. Sally didn't even know she was doing that. ▲

The concept "multi-tasking" isn't new; women have known about it for quite awhile. We do it all the time and aren't even aware of it. I can't convince you to do only one thing at a time, *all the time*, even if that's what the books recommend. Many of you take pride in being able to do several things at once.

I recall, as a child, watching a performer who could spin six plates on top of six poles, keeping them balanced simultaneously. As the orchestra played frenetic music, he'd dash from pole to pole, giving each plate a spin until finally, all of them spun in unison ...for about 15 seconds. It was an amazing sight.

He got paid to do this trick. How much do *you* get paid for doing six things at once?

What about gearing down to doing no more than *two* things at a time? It certainly would reduce that frenzied, scattered feeling you get when you're doing too much.

But, cutting back to two doesn't guarantee that you'll avoid multi-task disasters. Take the case of Mary Lou, who turned cooking supper into an episode right out of "I Love Lucy." She had cooked some pasta and steamed vegetables. After dumping the pasta into the colander and rinsing it with water, she added the vegetables. While the excess water drained, she got out a dispenser of liquid butter. (It was her habit to squirt a little on the pasta and vegetables just before serving them.)

At the same time, Mary Lou filled a plastic bin with hot water, preparing for her after-meal clean up. Two tasks, side by side in the sink. That's when she did a "Lucy."

Moving swiftly and confidently, she squirted *butter* into the *dishwater* and *dishwashing soap* onto the *pasta*!

If you do more than one thing at once, you need to pay close attention to *each* task. And as you perform each task, *stay in the moment*. Let's say you're eating a bowl of popcorn while watching television. Do you get so engrossed in the show, that you eat the whole bowl, *without remembering*

◄•••►

doing it? (If not popcorn, then how about ice cream, potato chips, a bowl of peanuts, just about any food eaten front of the TV?)

You see, our minds focus on one task at a time. So while we may have two going on, we can only track one at any particular moment. (A certain former president had trouble performing two tasks at once, remember?) And do you know why you were taught not to talk with your mouth full? It wasn't just to spare your table mates the sight of half-eaten food flopping around in your mouth. It was also to protect you from inhaling your food when you took a breath to speak!

Doing one thing at a time and focusing on it completely:

- Wards off forgetfulness
- Stabilizes your emotions
- Gives you greater mental energy because you're not fragmenting it
- Sharpens your senses and perceptions

Be careful what tasks you pair together—avoid drinking and driving, for example. And note what happens to your stress level as you try to give each task the attention it deserves. If you suffer for it or your results fall short of what you want, it's a sign that multi-tasking is not your best method for increasing your efficiency . . . or that you've combined the wrong tasks.

WHAT'S YOUR RUSH?

"**W**ho's Going to Make the Bed?" is the second longest-running argument in my marriage. ("Who's Doing the Cooking?" is the undefeated champion.)

121

◀••▶

My husband wants us to make our bed together each morning. I had stubbornly resisted all these years on the grounds that it made no sense to put *two* people on a *one*-person job.

This kind of thinking smacks of good business management. And it has no place in the bedroom.

So, after thirteen years, when he looked at me with those big brown eyes and said, "Honey, let's make the bed together. It's more fun that way," I *didn't* say, "Sorry. Making the bed is on the bottom of my fun-things-to-do-in-the-bedroom list." And I *didn't* restate my argument that "it's hard to justify *one* person making the bed, much less *two*."

Instead, I said "OK." My only request was that we buy one of those thick comforters you can throw over disheveled sheets and blankets, that makes the bed look like the picture in the catalog.

Now every morning, I cheerfully help Alan make the bed. But, the moment we finish, I sprint to the bathroom. When he knocks on the door and says, "Honey, let's shower together. It's more fun that way." I say, "Sorry, I've got to keep moving. But, why don't you start breakfast? It's more fun *that* way."

There's a moment when we feel the pace picking up. For me, it's right after I've indulged in our morning ritual of making the bed. When does it happen for you? Does it have to happen?

We're galvanized both by forces within us—the desire for high achievement, the wish to please loved ones, and the need to be dutiful—and those outside us. They include job requirements, community requests, society's pace, to name a few.

We tell ourselves we must meet both internal and external demands. And that's when we begin to rush, acting as though we can go faster and faster every millisecond of every day, impervious to weakness or fatigue.

These are the "time tyrants," the voices that shout in your head, *"Don't you have anything to do?! You're wasting valuable time! Get going!!"* all day long, every day.

They battle with the "time trainers," our reasonable and calm inner voices that say, "Take a break. Slow down. Rest a minute." Often, it's impossible to hear them above all the shouting.

The time tyrants often come out on top because they are fueled by a powerful chemical—adrenaline. These relentless voices cause us anxiety, which in turn produces a biochemical change that affects the brain, making us feel aroused and high. These are feelings we easily get used to and comfortable with. Soon, we become *addicted* to anxiously rushing about and the chemicals that it produces. So we continue to behave in ways that produce them.

What chances do the voices of reason have against this powerful chemical weapon? Pretty good, as it turns out. You start by asking yourself, "Why am I rushing?"

Some people satisfy their need for excitement by procrastinating. After all, crises are exhilarating. And there's nothing like a deadline to get adrenaline flowing.

◀••▶

When my daughter was young and I was a full-time mother, I used to save coupons. But, I think I must have been a little bored. Because I would purposely save them until the day they were going to expire, and then rush to the store to use them!

There are all kinds of adrenaline junkies. You've got drivers who constantly run yellow lights, endangering pedestrians and cars in their path. And then, you've got honest citizens like me who jaywalk now and then, because the light is taking too long to change. When Officer Michael J. Thornton of the Oakland P.D. showed no compassion and gave me a $24 ticket for sprinting across the street, I was cured of my addiction. (Who said thrills were cheap?)

Check yourself for these signs of time-pressured people outlined in the book, *Urgency Addiction: How to Slow Down Without Sacrificing Success,* by Nina Tass, Ph.D.

Do you go at too fast a pace? People who are time-driven constantly push themselves beyond their own comfort zone. Certain physical gestures betray this form of urgency: drumming fingers, darting and scanning eyes and a short attention span. (Walking into automatic doors before they open is another signal; not that I've had any personal experience with that . . .)

Do you monitor time excessively? You watch the clock closely and must always be near one or have a watch on your wrist. You live by a schedule, broken down to the quarter hour.

◄•••►

Do you say yes to all demands at work, resulting in longer hours? If long hours at work are an issue with loved ones, that's a sure sign that you're bowing to the pressures of a time-driven workplace.

Do you give up personal time? This act of self-deprivation is a frantic effort to meet unreasonable time demands. How much personal time have you set aside for yourself *each day*? (Women who manage stress well claim to take an average of 72 minute of time for themselves every day—that's a half hour more than those most beleaguered by stress, who manage only 40 minutes a day.)

Do you enjoy the present moment? Or, are you always focused on the future tasks that spread before you each day?

Contrast these traits with those of people who are at ease with time. They have an unerring sense of who they are in the flow of time. This gives them the self-confidence to resist the whims and worries of the moment. "Time-integrated" people share these traits. They:

1. never seem to be in a hurry.
2. experience the present moment to the fullest.
3. believe they deserve time for themselves.
4. make time to get what they want.
5. spend time on relationships that matter.
6. regard the past in a positive way—as a rich harvest of experience.
7. remain open and flexible.

◀••▶

In case you're thinking this is an exclusive club, it's not. I've witnessed the transformation of several time-trapped women into time-integrated ones. And each one told me that the healthy traits mentioned above were conscious and learned . . . over time.

MANAGE YOUR INVESTMENT WELL

Stop thinking about wasting time or spending time, or saving time. Instead, think about how you *invest* it. Put it where you'll get the highest personal return. Instead of scrambling to handle what's urgent, work within your rhythm on the right tasks.

The first step is one you cannot and must not skip. Sit down and think about what really matters—your basic values, goals, desires, and relationships. Decide what's important, what has the biggest payoff. As Stephen Covey says, "the key is not to prioritize your schedule, but to schedule your priorities."

You may decide, for example, that you need to re-negotiate your time with the people you live and work with. Especially if you have a habit of giving up time to allow other people to have more time for themselves—your boss, your co-workers, your partner, your children.

You start with two basic principles:

1. Everybody's time is intrinsically and equally valuable.
2. Household tasks don't have gender tags on them.

Now, working from those principles, you can redesign the way you invest your time, and devote more of it to yourself or the things that matter most.

Or, it's important to you to save your best energy for your family. As part of scheduling this priority, you need to consider how and when to do errands, a task that is probably on the bottom of your list.

Here's what a friend of mine does. She bundles errands. She calls it "doing the loop." By designating errands for her "low-energy" time of the day, when she needs to coast for awhile, she can engage in mindless relaxation. And to make her errands more enjoyable, she plays her favorite music in the car and sings along. She reserves the *right* type of mental energy for the *right* time of day and the *right* type of task. So, she arrives home feeling refreshed, rather than frazzled.

When you view your time as a wise investment, you're more likely to put your best energy where it's important, accept your limits, and accomplish your goal with less suffering.

Balance: *Soul Searching and Sole Soothing*

Up here on the balance beam, it's hard to take a break. But, you're going to be in serious trouble if you wait for someone to *give* it to you. A gymnast must recognize when she needs a break and take it, whether she's working with an Olympics coach, a boss at work, or caring for kids at home.

Here are four sure signs that you need to take more breaks more often:

1. You're moving faster than traffic (and you're on foot).
2. The last time you relaxed was when you were in the hospital being treated for exhaustion.
3. You think the Eveready Bunny® is lazy.
4. You haven't taken lunch away from your desk since 1985, and that was only because there was a power outage.

Siestas come from the ancient wisdom of pausing for several hours during the heat of the day. In our harried culture we would do well to aim for a "mini-siesta" several times a day.

Studies of peak performers have shown that people perform best when they can take a break from their work or routine every sixty to ninety minutes. Mini-breaks throughout the day are refreshing and re-energizing.

Macworld employees, who find they need a rest stop in the course of a day, can make use of a company-maintained nap room, according to a report in the *San Francisco Chronicle*. The "napatorium" has been in existence for 10 years, and offers sanitary and private sleeping conditions for two employees at a time. While many of the nappers keep a lower profile to avoid gossip within the company, the people who use it swear by it. One employee naps in mid-afternoon, after lunch and before coffee. She limits her nap to 20 minutes with a small alarm clock. "I could either spend the hours between 3 and 5 drowsy at my desk or shut my eyes and be productive."

THE PAUSE THAT REFRESHES

Society rewards the superperson. It takes practice to resist our conditioning to be perpetually busy and productive. It's all too easy to spend our days methodically crossing items off our to-do lists, fearing what might happen if we fail to fill every moment with "busy-ness."

Breaks help to relieve stress and recover your energy. They are terrific remedies for such common workplace maladies as tension, mental blocks, and the inability to focus.

Have you ever:

- reread several pages of a report that you daydreamed through?
- had to rewrite a poorly composed letter?
- had to refigure a column of numbers you miscalculated?
- apologized to an employee you snapped at because you were tired and frustrated?

If you have, then you know that it rarely works to keep pushing yourself. What you need is to stop and create the right kind of break for yourself.

If you've been sitting hunched over paper at your desk or glued to your phone, then stand up and stretch, take a walk down the hall and up a flight of stairs to jump start you metabolism, get your circulation going and get oxygen to your brain. This is particularly helpful if you're feeling sleepy or unmotivated.

Been concentrating for the last hour? Switch to something playful for a few minutes, such as reading comics, juggling, drawing, or playing computer games. It's like providing yourself with a mental kaleidoscope. Shake yourself up and you'll see the world and your problems differently.

Another way to get a break is to do deep breathing and positive imaging. Close your eyes for several minutes, and let your imagination take you to a place that means utter peace and sensual pleasure for you.

Look out the window and daydream. It's not wasted time, when done consciously and on purpose. And afterwards, you'll be more productive.

Shift tasks to give yourself a mental break. Go from creative thinking, such as brainstorming, illustrating, writing and teaching to something less taxing like filing or other administrative tasks. (I used this technique when I wrote this book, and it really works!)

Been working alone for many hours? Take a break to chat or laugh with someone else. Do the opposite if you've been in meetings all day. Take ten minutes by yourself.

When deciding how to time your breaks, take into account your work load, mental state, and physical condition that day. Two short breaks in the

◄••►

morning and two in the afternoon is probably fine. You can schedule them around the start and finish of energy-sapping activities. Consider your natural energy highs and lows. You may need more or fewer breaks. For example, if you're more of an afternoon or evening person, you may need to take 3 breaks in the morning. Then you'll soar through the afternoon on an energy high.

Linger an extra minute at lunch, in the powder room, and at your desk at the start and close of each day. It's another form of pausing that allows you to create transitions between activities. Do this religiously and you'll feel less rushed.

When you need to relax and you've only got a minute, briefly recall a pleasant experience or a time when you felt particularly relaxed. It seems like a small thing to do, but this technique calms you in a matter of seconds.

Remember, you deserve a break *each* day, several times a day. And don't think of breaks and work as two separate entities. They are part of a continuum of activities all geared toward accomplishing the day's goals.

- Get out of your office at least once a day if only for 10 minutes. Walk, smell the fresh air.
- Don't schedule yourself down to the minute.
- Leave 15 minute and half-hour breaks to make some notes and gather your thoughts.
- Alternate physical task with mental ones.
- Get control of the moment, take a deep breath, and think about something pleasant.

TA-DA! VS. TO-DO

Ta-Da [origin unknown]
1. vocal acknowledgment of an accomplishment, large or small. Best expressed in a gleeful voice with arms thrown wide. **2.** Also a sound computers make as they sign off. *Synonym:* "Hooray for me!" *Antonym:* To do.

When we get caught up in our to-do lists, checking off items in rapid succession, we forget the most important pause of all. It's the moment when we thank ourselves for a job well done.

Today, even computers acknowledge themselves when they finish their jobs. What's our excuse? Ta Da! may be the two most important words you say throughout the day. And to help you remember to say them, I suggest you convert your To-Do list to a Ta-Da! list. Simply write the word Ta-Da! at the top of your list or in the margin next to each item. Then, each time you complete a task, you'll glance down and see that a celebration is in order. Time to stand up, fling your arms wide and shout Ta-Da! Then, and only then, go on to the next item.

A MEASURE OF PLEASURE

Utne Reader magazine asked a lot of well-known people—Deepak Chopra, Jane Smiley, Richard Petty and Paula Wellstone among them—"How do you put on the brakes?" Most of them said they went out in nature, meditated, stopped looking at their e-mail, prayed, and slept a lot.

Now, these people could have spent a lot of money on a week in a ritzy spa or a vacation in the Bahamas, any number of luxurious pleasures.

But, notice that they selected simple ones.

If the idea of enjoying simple pleasures is new to you, or if you attach a dollar sign to pleasurable things and can't afford to give them to yourself, then it's time to start over.

Begin by asking yourself this crucial question: Which activities do you most enjoy simply because they bring you pleasure? Write down ten of your most favorite things to do, along with the last time you did them.

Remember that there are two kinds of pleasures: those that cost money and those that don't. Compare your list to these:

Pleasures that cost money:

1. Take yourself to the movies—alone.
2. Pick up a box lunch and take yourself on a picnic at a beautiful place.
3. Spend a few extra dollars and get your hair cut by a real hair designer.
4. Get your nails done, even if it's not a special occasion.
5. Buy a book that teaches you to do something that pleases you, like making flower arrangements.
6. Spend the night at a bed and breakfast inn by yourself.
7. Treat yourself to a recording of your favorite music.
8. Sign up for lessons to learn something you've always wanted to do—dancing, painting, piano, singing.
9. Hire someone to clean your house.

◄••►

10. Buy yourself a bouquet of flowers.
11. Enjoy a massage from a professional masseuse.
12. Get a professional facial.
13. Make an appointment with a makeup consultant.

(Adapted from *The Family Manager's Guide for Working Moms*, by Kathy Peel)

Pleasures that are free:

1. List ten things you do well.
2. Sing in the shower.
3. Hug someone.
4. Walk instead of ride.
5. Give yourself a compliment.
6. Keep a secret.
7. Practice courage in one small way.
8. Warm a heart.
9. Laugh at yourself.
10. Enjoy the silence.
11. Walk to the nearest park.
12. Surprise a child.
13. Pay a compliment.
14. Throw something away you don't like.
15. Waste a little time.
16. Curl up before an open fire with some cocoa.
17. Return something you've borrowed.
18. Think about droplets on rosebuds.

19. Organize some small corner of your life.
20. Pop popcorn.
21. Turn off the TV and talk.
22. Tell someone you love them.
23. Hold a hand.
24. Feed the ducks.
25. Pick up some travel brochures and dream.
26. Smell a flower.
27. Send a card to someone for no reason.
28. Take an early morning walk.
29. Tell someone how much you appreciate him/her.
30. Look into the heart of a flower.
31. Look at old photos.
32. Encourage a young person.
33. Follow an impulse.
34. Visit a lonely person.
35. Listen to the rain on the roof.
36. Acknowledge when you are wrong.
37. Volunteer some time to a good cause.
38. Give yourself a present.
39. Have breakfast in bed.
40. Let someone do you a favor.
41. Reread a favorite book.
42. Give a dog a bone.
43. Allow yourself to make another mistake.

(From *47 Presents to Give Yourself*; Mission: AIDS Volunteer Manual)

◄••►

Feel free to borrow ideas from these lists. Keep a copy of your "Favorite Pleasures" list at your office and at home. Then, the next time you don't know what to do with your leisure time, instead of ending up in front of the television, you can choose from a multitude of choices, custom-designed for you!

The Harris survey reports that the amount of leisure time enjoyed by the average American has shrunk 37% since 1973. Over the same period, the average work week, including commute time has jumped from under 41 hours to nearly 47 hours. This means our ability to find simple pleasures in each day is critical.

Don't save your enjoyment for the weekends and holidays. Find something to enjoy each day, something that makes you laugh and celebrate. A kindness, an achievement—be it large or small—a smell, a sound, a touch. These are daily joys that we must savor, like a rich piece of chocolate or a balmy summer evening.

ARE YOU IMMUNE TO LIFE'S PLEASURES?

Arthur Stone, psychologist from State University of New York, found that pleasant events gave a boost to the immune system that lasted for two to three days. In contrast, a stressful event like an argument with a boss or spouse slightly depressed the immune system for a day. He concluded that the *absence* of ordinary pleasures, like a walk in the woods or an evening with friends, may take an even greater toll on our health than stress does.

We all go through periods when we feel at best, ho-hum, and at worst, just plain awful about ourselves. Sometimes these episodes are triggered by a specific crisis. But more often, it is the sad but logical result of years of neglect or mistreatment.

When we're feeling worthless, we tend to reject the very things that would help us feel better—unpressured time to write a letter, read a good book, relax in the sun, visit with a friend, or just do nothing.

If these feelings get in the way of your enjoying life's abundant pleasures, then try keeping a log to measure your progress. Record your answers to these questions daily:

1. What was one thing I enjoyed today?
2. What would I like to do differently tomorrow?
3. What is one thing I accomplished today?
4. What is one thing I'm looking forward to?
5. What was my energy level on a scale of 1-10?

Keeping this log will show you there is movement, even if your notes seem to be about trivial things. These are the tiny steps that lead to amazing leaps.

THE NEW "LADY OF LEISURE"

Are you overprogrammed? Is leisure time no longer a relaxing break from routine? Check for these signs:

- Weekends booked full—shopping, family obligations, with little or no free time for spontaneous activities.

- Feeling anxious when nothing is scheduled during leisure time.
- Taking short, active vacations.
- Staying in touch with the office while on vacation.
- Scheduling numerous activities for leisure time.
- Playing as hard as you work.
- Placing a high value on being busy, even during leisure time.
- Feeling like recreation is just another job to do.

Technology may also be an enemy when it comes to "down time" because it's so easy to remain "plugged in" by fax, e-mail, mobile phone, and pager. According to a *Newsweek* article called "Taking Off, Tuning In," these devices blur the boundaries between office and home, and office and vacation. The advances that were supposed to free people often turn into digital shackles. "You're on a remote beach in Waikiki; you've got mail." When we transfer the hectic pace and get-ahead attitude of the business world to our leisure lives, we derive no real benefit from leisure or play.

If you want to take more leisure time or build simple pleasures into each day, you must start by learning to trust yourself. Trust that if you relax a bit, you won't drop out or become a failure. Recognize each chance for unmanaged time and take it exuberantly.

THE POWER OF LAUGHTER AT HOME AND WORK

There is a great deal of evidence that one of the best ways to maintain a balanced perspective is to have a good sense of humor. That doesn't mean being a clown or a jokester. It means having the ability to see the non-serious element in everyday situation when it just isn't going right.

Adventures In Gymnastics

When my daughter was eight months old, my two sisters came to visit. We were sitting around the kitchen table one afternoon, while I was nursing Lauren. When I finished, my sister placed her in the bouncy seat on the floor.

My outfit of choice during that period was bib overalls, because I could unhook the shoulder straps to nurse. For some reason, I can't remember why, I stood up. But, my overalls stayed seated; I'd forgotten to refasten the shoulder straps.

There I stood in the in the middle of the kitchen with my overalls around my knees. "Whoops," was all I could think of to say, as my sisters howled with laughter.

They didn't just get a kick out of seeing me so exposed; they were having trouble breathing. My younger sister went into the dining room to try to stop laughing. It didn't help. Meanwhile, my older sister rolled around on the kitchen floor, gasping for air. I sat back down, so weak from laughing, I couldn't even pull up my pants.

Then suddenly, from the bouncy seat came the sound of a baby laughing. Lauren was *laughing at us*. She thought *we* were funny! Her giggles set off a second round of laughter, even louder than the first.

◄••►

Every time we quieted down, hoping to catch our breath, Lauren giggled again, totally incapacitating us. It was like she was saying, "Hey! Don't stop now! This party's just getting started!" We were completely at her mercy.

That day we set the record for the longest laugh in my family's history; it took nearly 10 minutes for us to pull ourselves together, not including the time it took me to get dressed. And it all started because something didn't go just right. ▲

Having a good sense of humor and having fun at work will help you stay healthy, live longer and be more creative, satisfied and productive, too. According to Steve Wilson, author of *Eat Dessert First,* it's a good idea to integrate a sense of play throughout your work day. Jokes via e-mail; funny pens or desk toys are good. Personalize your work space with things that make you chuckle or smile.

And if you're planning some department or company-wide fun, here are some good guidelines:

- Keep it fresh.
- Keep it inoffensive.
- Keep it meaningful.

For example, at one IBM unit, they tear down organizational barriers by having top executives do an employee's job for a day, with the employee supervising. Also, they encourage employees to bring in their children to participate for the 15-minute morning sing-along.

When I work with companies, I promote teamwork by having a group form the Toot Your Talent Chorus™. Instead of serenading their co-workers with singing, they play kazoos. One group chose to march through the halls playing "Oh, When the Saints Go Marching In." Two entire departments got up from their desks and followed them, creating a spontaneous parade.

There's a good reason why there's a movement to integrate work and play in companies today. It reduces stress. And if you're waiting until you finish your work to find time to play, remember this: You will never finish all your work, even when you die.

Stay open to the absurd and the silly. It will keep you smiling during the tense times. Reclaim some time for pure play and pure enjoyment. It doesn't have to be lots of time. Nor should you run away from any of your responsibilities. Just be on the lookout for minutes you can steal for pleasure.

As Steve Wilson reminds us, "In all the recorded history of medicine there is no evidence that anyone has actually 'died laughing' but, the term 'dead serious' is something we'd better think about."

A CHEESEBURGER IS NOT FOOD FOR THE SOUL

Do you take certain times of the week to self-nurture? Ideally, would you like to have more time by yourself, less time, or are you satisfied with the amount of time you are by yourself these days? Thirty-one percent of people polled in a recent study said they want more alone time and only 6% said they wanted less.

◄••►

Many people have lost the knack for being alone, and so are actually uncomfortable when they suddenly have unexpected time. Thinking about your average seven-day week, how many of your waking hours are you by yourself each week?

I can take a leisurely bath and not be disturbed, because my family has learned that this is sacred time for me. But, if I want more than that, it's hard to justify it to both myself and others. *Because being alone comes perilously close to looking like you're being selfish*. But being appropriately selfish is a very healthy thing to do. There's an extremely valuable restorative power in being alone.

Nourishing yourself mentally, emotionally, and spiritually means unplugging from the world, pampering yourself, making no demands on your mind, staring into space, daydreaming . . . *alone*.

We must take time to replenish ourselves and our souls each day or we will come to a crashing halt; if not now, eventually. Women assume caregiving roles more often than men and need time alone and away from the people they care for. It took me a long time to understand that I needed solitary time to think and reflect.

Mothers of young children tell me that they feel like they're doing well just taking a shower in the morning and getting out now and then without the stroller. One mother discovered her enemy—guilt. (Sound familiar?) She felt compelled not to squander those hours away from her children on herself. She thought that time should yield tangible results. "It's hard to use up precious baby-sitting hours accomplishing nothing concrete," she said.

Elaine St. James, author of *Simplify Your Life*, suggests that you calendar alone time and offers other strategies for finding nuggets of solitude:

1. Stay up 30 minute later—or wake up early.
2. Don't use your kids' nap time for work. Make their quiet time your quiet time.
3. Swap kids. "I'll take yours Monday if you take mine Friday."

Author and mother, Christina Baker Kilens, who suffered from guilt over wanting and needing alone time, worked to reshape that time to fit her real needs. Now, when the sitter comes, before she does anything else, she sometimes spends a half hour at a coffee bar writing in a notebook. Sometimes she sits by the river.

She shares some of her post-guilt experiences:

"I've conducted little mental exercises, uncovering aspects of my life that might bear exploration, like feelings that gnaw at me, worries about money, all the different hats I wear, and how they converge to create my identity. As I reframe and refine my understanding of who I am and who I want to become, I'm learning to value what's important and let go of the rest."

Time disappears when I'm writing. I'm constantly amazed to look up and see that two hours have passed. I wasn't aware of even one minute. It's as though I were suspended in time and space.

Where is your place or what is your activity, where time is not on your mind? Where do you enter another world where you feel wonder and total

◀••▶

peace? Is it out in your garden? Walking along the beach? Staring at the clouds? These are time-free zones that nourish us and soothe us. How many do you have in your life?

Spiritual and emotional nourishment often overlap. Because spirituality is woven into the fabric of our lives, feeling nurtured spiritually will carry over into all other areas of life. We find spiritual nourishment from many sources. For me, it's from forests and streams. Also, it's sounds like beautiful voices singing, or a fog horn, or a child's laughter. Take time to notice all these sources of healing.

THE CARE AND FEEDING OF THE GYMNAST'S SOUL

Step One: Sit quietly for five minutes each day.

Step Two: Let your own voice speak to you. (Time-driven people silence the sound of their inner selves; give your voice room to speak.)

Step Three: Settle down get past the mental static in your mind. Use any method that works for you—videos, audio tapes, deep breathing.

Step Four: Descend into the core of your self, where the sense of being at one with the flow of time awaits you.

Sacred time alone helps you prioritize and realign what matters. And it helps you develop inner trust, pay attention your body's signals and listen to gentler, more reasonable voices that you keep in your head. As you learn to hear your deeper self, you'll trust your ability to flow with your own individual temperament. Gradually, you'll discover what is important to you,

◄•••►

what you need to make more time for, and what it feels like to be in balance with yourself and the world.

Balance: *Taking Your Fear To New Heights*

On a trip to Toronto with my daughter, we visited the tallest single standing tower in the world, the CNN building, where you could walk over a glass floor and view the ground hundreds of feet below. Wanting to be a good role model, I took Lauren by the hand, and said, "Let's do it! It's perfectly safe."

She ended up dragging me across the floor like an unwilling dog on a leash, while I covered my eyes and screamed. Afterwards she crossed that looming precipice over and over, taunting me with "What's so hard about this, Mom?"

Some gymnasts are lucky enough to be born without a fear of heights. Others aren't so fortunate. But, no matter. Every gymnast can conquer her fear of heights, with the right motivation. (If Mel Gibson was waiting for me across that glass abyss, I'd forget my fear and run into his arms, in about three seconds.)

Each gymnast sees the four feet between her and the floor differently. It's a matter of perception: what represents a big risk to you, might not be a big risk for someone else.

Perhaps you're one of those people who face each challenge with excitement and enthusiasm. You might be a high risk taker. Stimulation and lots of it, plus variety and intensity are the qualities you seek. You enjoy challenges, often with a hint of danger in them. You'll need to learn a little more caution on the balance beam: practice with a spotter, move slowly until you've mastered the move and don't try reckless stunts.

Or, maybe the idea of being on the balance beam causes you dread and anxiety. You are probably a low risk taker. You'd prefer to keep your feet on the ground and avoid any possibility of unsteadiness. Analyzing a diagram of how to do a forward flip, rather than going out there and performing one, is far more attractive. To function well up here, you'll need to limit the amount of information you seek. Otherwise, you'll forget to take the risk. So, repeat after me:

One for the money.
Two for the show.
Three to get ready.
Three to get ready.
Three to get ready . . .

"Don't forget the "Four to go's!" says speaker, Rosita Perez, who quotes the wisdom of Gestalt therapy founder, Fritz Perls.

Low risk takers and high risk takers balance each other out. And when they don't work together on important projects, the results can be disastrous.

Associated Press newsflash from Arvada, Colorado: "A man killed during a bungee jump was attached to a cord that was 70 feet too long."

If you were going to make a bungee jump, wouldn't you want a meticulous *low* risk taker measuring the length of the cord?! It takes all kinds of

◄•••►

gymnasts *working together* to live up here.

One type of risk taker is no better than another. Each type is based on temperament, genetics, and emotional and mental health. I'm a combination risk taker. I take big risks in some areas of my life and no, or few risks in other areas. For example, I will gladly speak before 1000 people, but I won't go scuba diving.

Our most successful risks tend to be the ones where we have the innate ability or developed skill to perform well. But, planning and preparation account for a big part of our success, too. Without them you're not taking a *risk*, you're taking a *chance*. And there's a big difference.

You can learn to succeed at just about anything, with the right combination of information, support, and training.

HOW TO BECOME A SUCCESSFUL RISK TAKER

- Identify what kind of risk taker you are. Work *with* your type, not against it.
- If you're a high risk taker, ask yourself: "What's the *best* thing that could happen if I acted now, with the information I have?" And remember what Henry David Thoreau said. "If you've built castles in the air, your work need not be lost. That is where they should be. Now build the foundation beneath them."
- If you're a low risk taker, ask yourself: "What's the *worst* thing that could happen if I took this risk?" Then develop a mental plan to

deal with the imagined consequences. You'll feel more confident about moving forward.

- If you can't motivate yourself to take risks, you may be depressed. Get some help. Depression is a common problem that can be treated with good results.
- Spend time with healthy risk takers. Watch and learn from them.
- Keep a victory log. It's hard to dispute solid evidence.

Risk taking is action based on self-esteem. In other words, at some points in our lives, self-esteem is something we *do*. Positive action—like walking a balance beam with confidence—empowers us. Even a seemingly trivial accomplishment can inspire optimism and a desire to carry on.

Balance: *Keep Your Eye On That Spot On The Wall*

Every gymnast knows this as sure as she knows her own name. If you get dizzy, if you're performing a complex acrobatic move, if you need to maintain your focus, *keep your eye on that spot on the wall*.

Stay focused on the quality of time spent with people you love, and doing the things and activities you love. If you have people in your life who are not supportive, with whom you have little in common, or who never reciprocate, don't dilute your focus by spending time with them.

Remember why you're up here. You chose this life for the richness and texture it offers, as well as for its complexities.

Nurture the healing dimensions of life. Cultivate self-awareness and closeness with others.

Establish a core set of values. They will be your guiding star when your direction seems unclear.

Live your values and truths. Be true to yourself and you will be true to others. Before you say "yes" to something or someone, ask yourself: "If I had only one more year to live, would I still say 'yes'?"

Operate from a position of strength and power . . . and compassion.

Focus on the elements in life that bring you the most satisfaction.

10% of everything in life is truly important. Manage the other 90% well, so that it doesn't spill over into what really counts.

Take on something only after you have given up something else. Even Ta-Da! lists can get overloaded if you don't follow the "add one, subtract another" rule.

Aim for balance in these areas of your life:

- Work
- Relationships
- Family
- Spiritual and personal growth
- Leisure time
- Alone time
- Contributions
- Hobbies

Keep your eye on that spot on the wall. And . . . it helps if you don't look down.

GRACE

Amazing Leaps

Grace: *Forward Springs and Backward Flips*

Did you ever wonder why Olympic judges score gymnasts on both technical merit and style? And why a gymnast can score lower than her competitors in her technical performance and still win a medal? Because the judges place the same weight on performing with grace as they do on performing with accuracy. Grace and individual style are valued in the Olympics, in life, and on the balance beam.

My daughter, Lauren, is not a little girl anymore. It hit me the day the salesperson gently steered me out of the Children's Department last fall, saying, "I know it's a shock. But, it happens to every mother." I was about to say that the store should have given me more time to prepare or, at least, sent me a letter, when I saw my daughter prancing down the aisle toward the Juniors Department.

There she was, looking at posters of come-hither models wearing short skirts, tiny little tops, and too much makeup. I looked back at the children's department one last time and hurried to catch up with her. I've been trying to keep up ever since.

For example, I've been secretly preparing for the day a boy asks her out. After she's asleep, I sneak down to my office to work on my new web site called www.date.com. This is my clearinghouse for all her potential suitors. Any boy who wants to date my daughter must first complete an application.

It will ask revealing questions like, "How many parts of your body are pierced? Which ones are they?" and "What contraceptive product got its name from the story of Helen of Troy?" (If he's not smart enough to get that answer right, he's not smart enough to date my daughter.) Then, each boy must submit a 500-word essay on the benefits of safe sex. By the time he's finished, my daughter will be nearly 21. *That's* when I'll start to worry.

Until then, I'm going to adopt these rules for surviving her teen years:

- Be open to new things.
- Avoid embarrassing her.
- Choose my battles wisely.
- Allow her to practice her independence.
- Listen.
- Let her paint my nails any color she chooses.

No doubt, I'll feel ambivalent about every leap she makes. But, ambivalence is part of being human. One moment we do forward springs across the balance beam. The next, backward flips. Don't worry. We still earn points if we do them with grace.

Grace: *And You Thought You Didn't Have It In You!*

Do you express yourself creatively and enrich others in the process? If your answer is "yes," then you can read this section with one eye closed. Because, you've already got half of my message.

But, if you're not sure what it means to express yourself creatively and in a way that adds grace to your life, then keep both eyes open. Understand, I'm not talking about artistic ability, though it's nice to have some talent in that area. You don't have to sing, dance, or paint; what you need is the freedom and courage to use your imagination.

Take Mary, for example, head of a work and family center at a large hospital. For months she had been campaigning for a Lactation Room where mothers could nurse in private. After begging for space with no positive results, she came up with this imaginative approach. She found a large storage closet that could comfortably seat three women at a time. Then she started circulating memos about the "Milk of Human Kindness Award," a special citation that would be presented at the opening of the hospital's Lactation Room. To be eligible, all you had to do was donate an item to make the room warm and inviting, like a painting or a comfortable chair.

On opening day, over 50 staff showed up. Milk and cookies and other dairy snacks were served. Internal publicity photos were taken. And of

◄••►

course, the air was buzzing with who would win the coveted award.

Mary is no Michelangelo or Mozart. But she has a gift for using her imagination in ways that benefit everyone.

To live our lives with grace, we must find the best parts of ourselves and express them. Many women have lost their creative gifts along the way. Some misplaced them while caring for others. (One mother I know gave up creative writing, her passion, until her children left for college.)

And then there are those who hide their creativity behind protective armor. They say things like, "Oh, I'm not very creative" or "I don't have any talent." This is never the case. Each of us is born creative with a rich imagination, just waiting to be tapped.

Maurice Freehill asks, "Who is more foolish? The boy afraid of the dark or the man afraid of the light?" Are you afraid of the light? Are you afraid to see who you really are? There is no substitute for self knowledge. Only by shining the light on your innermost thoughts and feelings will your rich creative gifts reveal themselves.

Think of yourself as a miner at the bottom of a deep shaft. At first, there's only darkness. But turn on your head lamp and chip away at the layers of rock, and you'll find the precious gems beneath.

◄••►

CREATIVITY ON TAP

A well-known study showed that there are certain activities during which people get their best ideas. The top three are:

3. While driving in the car

2. While showering

1. While sitting on the toilet

This information could be applied by managers seeking innovative ideas from their employees. Some creative recommendations I've made to major corporations include:

- Move brainstorming sessions to your favorite bathroom stall.
- Make sure there are pads of note paper and a supply of pencils near each toilet.
- Install showers in each bathroom. Offer incentives for coming to work dirty, and encourage employees to shower during office hours.
- Replace office time with driving time. Provide small tape recorders for employees to capture their ides as they drive around. (If they get as far as Las Vegas or Disney World, review the policy.)

Humor often gives us access to our best solutions. A study by Dr. Alice Isen at Cornell University, found that people who had just seen a funny movie had a "creative flexibility" that wasn't evident two hours earlier.

◄··►

To help people access their creative flexibility, I have them do this exercise. Each person picks a partner. Then they turn to their partner and tell her a *bold-faced lie*.

I'll never forget the two nurses who brought the house down, when they stepped up to the microphone in front of 1500 people. I asked them, "What lie did you tell each other?"

First woman: "I said I was a virgin."

Second woman: "I said, 'I believe you.'"

Adventures In Gymnastics

A few months ago my friend, Sherry told me a dirty secret about her oven. She hadn't cleaned it in five years. My first reaction was to laugh. I hadn't used my oven since my daughter was six years old, and that was only to harden her clay creations. Open the door today and you'll see a Play Doh® graveyard, filled with the grotesque remains of giraffes and elephants that couldn't take the heat.

"Get a self-cleaning oven," I told her. "And don't look back." When she didn't latch on to my idea, I was stumped. Why would such an accomplished woman agonize over the condition of a kitchen appliance?

Three weeks went by, and I thought I'd heard the last about her oven. Then, in the mail, came a most unusual invitation. It was an invitation to join the Easy-Off® Support Group.

On the designated Saturday afternoon, a group of Sherry's nearest and dearest friends arrived at her home, not knowing what to expect. As we walked through her front door, the smell of Easy-Off® was impossible to miss. On the beautifully set kitchen table were personalized oven-cleaning gloves for each of us. (Martha Stewart would have been proud.) And, there was Sherry with her head in the oven, laughing and saying, "Thanks for coming. I couldn't have faced this mess without you!"

During the afternoon the conversation turned to jobs we dreaded or avoided. One woman came up with a creative solution to our backed-up projects. She proposed that on a bi-monthly basis, our group meet at a selected member's home. The host would choose an overdue chore that she didn't want to face alone. And the group would help her get it done. We could swap our collective shame for camaraderie. It was brilliant!

Today our group serves the same purpose as the barn raisings and quilting bees did 100 years ago. Only now, you'll find us in dusty attics or an overgrown gardens. We've painted, hammered, bagged, and hauled. We've triumphed over tasks that somehow got overblown in our minds. And, we've accepted each other's help with grace. Our motto is *Fight Grime Without Guilt!* ▲

Our infinite ability to come up with creative solutions to seemingly insurmountable tasks makes me want to leap and dance for joy. To all of you who use your gifts wisely and gracefully, I do a handspring, two forward flips and a pirouette.

Grace: *Plant Your Feet Firmly*

How many of you are perfectionists? You wouldn't necessarily know it if you were. Here are some behaviors that should tip you off:

- You make all your kids' water from scratch.
- You do the Sunday crossword puzzle with an ultrafine pen and a bottle of correction fluid, so that you can neatly fix mistakes.
- You never have a bad hair day.

Julia Cameron, author of *The Artist's Way: A Spiritual Path to Higher Creativity*, writes: "Perfectionism is not a quest of the best. It is a pursuit of the worst in ourselves, the part that tells us that nothing we do will ever be good enough . . ."

It is in the learning and trying that we experience life. When we succeed, it's a wonderful moment that becomes ours to treasure always. But imperfect moments can be just as rich and memorable.

Last year I appeared on the Oprah Winfrey show, an exciting milestone in my career as an author and a speaker. I was on stage for 17 minutes(!) in front of a live audience and millions of viewers.

As the broadcast day drew nearer, my nervousness grew. What if I'd said something stupid? What if I looked fat? I did the only thing a mature, grown women could do. I made my husband come home from work to watch the show with me.

Alan, Lauren and I piled into our king-sized bed, with me in the middle. I held the covers up to my chin and warned them, "If I hate it, I'm going to hide under the covers and never come out." They agreed that would be a reasonable thing to do. We tuned in to watch.

Right before my segment, an educator by the name of Ann Lindquist spoke about teaching sex education to children. Then I came on. Oprah introduced me, flashed a photo of my book, and began the interview. About five minutes into it, a graphic appeared at the bottom of the screen. It identified me as "Ann Lindquist, Sex Educator." My big moment, and *nobody knew it was me*!

After the broadcast, my publicist called the producer to straighten things out. The producer promised that if the show was re-broadcast, the correct graphic would appear. A few months later they re-ran the show, and my name was Paula Statman again. I was happy.

Then several months later my segment appeared in a show called "The Best of Oprah." I was thrilled to be included! I just wished that I—instead of Ann Lindquist—had appeared. You guessed it. They had used the master copy with the mistake in it again. This time I had to laugh. One of the crowning moments in my career, and I wasn't even there to enjoy it!

This wonderfully imperfect, and humbling experience gave me the impetus to send this book to Oprah, just in case she wants to have me on the show again. In the meantime, Ann, if a producer calls you, please give them my phone number. And, by the way, you did a great job.

◀ •• ▶

THE GRACEFUL DISMOUNT

Remember the mechanic's bill that's hanging on my office wall, reminding me to not burn out my engine or myself? I'm happy to say that by 1995, I had gained a little wisdom and had mended some of my ways. I wrote this poem to show that there's hope for all of us, even compulsive over-achievers like me. Now I share it with you, with my deep gratitude for the time we've spent together up here . . . on the balance beam.

◄••►

Balance

We are creating history.
More than ever before, we are our own role models.
We are re-examining our roles, rules and responsibilities.
We do this to create new realities where we need them most.
In our society, in our relationships and within ourselves.
We are paving the way for the future by asking questions that
until now were unaskable, by challenging assumptions that
until now were not ours to challenge.
We need to dance to our own rhythm and not march to a beat
that pounds away at us.
We need to expect what is reasonable from ourselves and tame
that tyrant within who accepts nothing short of perfection.
We can trust the part of ourselves that is wise and true.
It will guide us if we let it be heard about the
commotion in our lives.
We need the skill to negotiate, the power to delegate, and the
courage to let go.
For it is in letting go that we discover our richest inner treasures.
And we finally learn that balance is not an item on our to-do list.
Balance is an art.
It is the art of imperfection.

—Paula Statman
© Copyright 1995

ON THE SAFE SIDE

The award-winning book
by Paula Statman

Featured on **Oprah** and the **Today Show,** and selected by a book of the month club, this is the book that earned Paula Statman an international reputation as a pioneer in the field of personal safety education.

Learn how to teach kids to deal with *all* kinds of people in potentially dangerous situations, and help them avoid becoming victims. Paula's groundbreaking approach—a blend of practical information and easy-to-teach tools—gives parents and professionals the skills and confidence to deal with this difficult subject. If you want more peace of mind, and you buy only one book on this subject, *On The Safe Side* is the one to get. Available in English and Spanish.

Order directly through the KidWISE Institute, Inc. by sending $12.00 plus $4.00 shipping and handling (checks and money orders only, please) to: 484 Lake Park Ave. #101, Oakland, CA 94610. Credit card orders call 1-800-300-9800.

Order **both** *Life on a Balance Beam* and *On the Safe Side* for $20.00! Offer available only through the KidWISE Institute.

About the Author

Paula Statman is a sought-after lecturer and the founder of the KidWISE Institute in Oakland, California. A mental health expert and educator for over twenty years, she has earned an international reputation in the field of personal growth and parent education. She presents over 50 programs a year and frequently appears on national media. Paula lives in Oakland with her husband and daughter.